BOOK 4
COMPETING WITH CAPABILITIES

BOOK 5
CHOOSING A STRATEGY

BOOK 6
STRATEGY AND INNOVATION

MBA
Strategy

The Open University

BUSINESS SCHOOL

The Open University,
Walton Hall, Milton Keynes MK7 6AA

First published 1996. Second edition 1998. Reprinted with amendments 1999

Copyright © 1998 The Open University

All rights reserved. No part of this work may be reproduced, stored in a retrieval system or transmitted, in any form or by any means, without written permission from the publisher or a licence from the Copyright Licensing Agency Ltd. Details of such licences (for reprographic reproduction) may be obtained from the Copyright Licensing Agency Ltd, 90 Tottenham Court Road, London W1P 0LP.

Edited, designed and typeset by The Open University

Printed in the United Kingdom by Henry Ling Limited, The Dorset Press, Dorchester, Dorset DT1 1HD

ISBN 0 7492 8995 3

Further information on Open University Business School courses may be obtained from the Course Sales Development Centre, The Open University, PO Box 222, Milton Keynes MK7 6YY (Telephone: 01908 653449).

oubs.open.ac.uk

BOOK 4

COMPETING WITH CAPABILITIES

Author: Susan Segal-Horn

MBA Strategy

Contents

1 Introduction — 5
  1.1 Learning objectives of this book — 6
  1.2 What is the resource-based approach to strategy? — 7
  1.3 The value chain concept and its relationship to capabilities — 10

2 Why do organisations differ? — 14
  2.1 Resources and capabilities as sources of advantage — 15
  2.2 Conceptual analysis of the sources of advantage — 16
  2.3 The role of know-how, tacit knowledge and human resources — 21

3 Resources and capabilities — 26
  3.1 The economics of strategy: markets or hierarchies — 27
  3.2 The economics of multi-product or multi-business organisations — 30
  3.3 Grant's five-stage model — 31
  3.4 The role of organisational routines and learning in building and transferring capabilities — 35
  3.5 Capabilities and change — 40

4 The boundaries of the organisation — 42
  4.1 Corporate strategy issues: organisations or 'virtual' organisations? — 42
  4.2 Dynamic capabilities issues: building organisational capability — 44
  4.3 Ownership, control or just links in a chain? — 47

5 Summary and conclusion — 48
  5.1 Objectives revisited — 48

References — 49

Acknowledgements — 51

1 Introduction

Strategy is concerned with the question of how organisations achieve and sustain superior performance. If they are commercial firms, then superior performance over time is based on sources of competitive advantage. If they are not-for-profit organisations, superior performance may be judged in a great variety of ways. A school may be judged by examination pass rates; a hospital may assess numbers of patients treated and unit cost of treatment; the police service may use crime detection rates; charities may look at funds raised and projects successfully supported by those funds; and so on. Whatever the mission and objectives of your organisation, strategic management provides analytical frameworks which enable it to focus its resources on achieving superior performance.

In Book 3, our discussion focused on understanding the external environment. It showed how organisations must monitor, interpret and make sense of the macro-economic environment, the industry environment and the competitive environment in order to grow or, sometimes, simply in order to survive. In this book, we shift the emphasis from the external to the internal context of strategy: the resources that the organisation possesses, or may need to possess, as the basis of robust strategy. It thus requires a shift in the unit of strategic analysis, from the industry (or public or voluntary sectors) to the organisation. 'Competing with Capabilities' suggests that opportunities emerge from an organisation's unique capabilities. This uniqueness arises not from the resources put into them, which are likely to be broadly similar to those of comparable organisations, but from the way they are used. Therefore strategic analysis must be able to look in detail at each organisation and identify:

- what its capabilities are
- how relevant they are to the objectives of the organisation
- what new capabilities may be needed over time
- how to build them internally or acquire them from elsewhere.

Broadly speaking, then, capabilities are the means by which organisations implement their strategies.

Organisations may have the same resources but different capabilities. Any asset which exists in an organisation constitutes a resource: buildings, systems, people, equipment, technology, finance, etc. Daft (1983) has suggested that resources are all assets, capabilities, organisational processes, controlled information or knowledge which enable that organisation to develop and implement strategies that improve its efficiency and effectiveness. This confuses the important difference between resources and capabilities. Capabilities are the outcome of using groups of resources in particular ways (Amit and Schoemaker, 1993; Grant, 1991). Grant argues:

> There is a key distinction between resources and capabilities. Resources are inputs into the production process – they are the basic units of analysis. ... But, on their own, few resources are productive. Productive activity requires the co-operation and co-ordination of teams of resources. A capability is the capacity for a team of resources to perform some task or activity. While resources are the source of a firm's

capabilities, capabilities are the main source of its competitive advantage.

(pp. 118–9)

Such 'teams' of resources are certainly not just human teams. They are any combination of the mixture of buildings, systems, people, equipment, finance or technology listed above. In Book 3 you were given quite detailed insight into how the management of financial resources by efficient managers can result in combining total resources in a different way. The Electrolux–Zanussi case analysis looked at levels of debt, asset management (especially the rise in fixed assets and its impact on capacity-utilisation) and analysis of the cost chain and its impact on margins. It then showed the relationships between all these financial management issues and the overall potential resource cluster of Electrolux and the impact on Electrolux's strategic options. Different financial and managerial resources are an essential part of this range of possible resource *clusters*, the combining of which makes different organisations different.

These issues are central to both business and not-for-profit organisations. The *resource-based* approach to strategy provides a perspective on the design and implementation of strategies over time which focuses attention on management actions which are relevant across all sectors.

1.1 LEARNING OBJECTIVES OF THIS BOOK

This book is about strategy at the level of the organisation. This section lays out the definitions and ideas behind the main concepts in this book. Section 2 considers the apparently simple question – why are organisations in the same sector different from each other? Section 3 is in two parts: a set of discussion sub-sections which define further some of the concepts in the resource-based perspective; and a mini-case on an international company to illustrate capability building as a long-term process. Finally, in Section 4, we look at what the resource perspective implies for the size, scope and functions of organisations. Where should the boundaries be drawn?

After studying this book you should be able to:

- demonstrate that strategy should include creating and maintaining resources and the structures in which to use them
- describe the resource-based view of the organisation as an approach to strategy, complementing the industry structure and environmental analysis approach to competitive strategy
- state the difference between a resource and a capability
- describe how organisations in the same sector may be able to develop and sustain different types of advantage from different clusters of capabilities
- identify critical resources and any distinctive capabilities for organisations, including your own
- describe the dynamic relationship between change in an industry or sector and corresponding change in organisational resources and capabilities
- demonstrate that capability building is a long-term process.

1.2 WHAT IS THE RESOURCE-BASED APPROACH TO STRATEGY?

The resource-based view of the firm has emerged as an approach which explores an important set of ideas (see Prahalad and Hamel, 1990; Barney, 1991; Peteraf, 1993). At its heart is the idea that all organisations possess unique bundles of assets, and that such 'ownership' of these bundles of assets, together with the use the firm is able to make of them, determines the difference in performance between one organisation and another, in the same sector. This also means that it is an approach to strategy which emphasises the role of managers in determining how well or poorly they use the assets which their organisations possess.

It must be stressed that in this book we are progressing from strategic thinking at the level of industries and industry or sector analysis, towards strategic thinking at the level of the organisation. The resource-based perspective on which we focus is not about reviewing the attractiveness of entire industries and their profit and growth potential for new entrants, it is about what individual organisations can do to understand themselves better. It gives attention to skills and 'know-how' that organisations may take for granted. It sees capabilities as things that must be developed and built over time. Even if 'bought' as part of an acquisition, getting the old and new resources to work together to produce an enhanced capability (often described as a 'synergy' at the time of a merger) is itself dependent on the organisational capability to integrate two sets of resources post-acquisition. This point was illustrated by the Electrolux–Zanussi case analysed in Book 3, where Electrolux's post-acquisition management expertise is clearly an important capability which was critical in achieving the effective integration of the resources of the two companies.

From this perspective then, strategy is about 'choosing among and committing to long-term paths or trajectories of competence development' (Teece *et al.*, 1990 p. 38). These authors call this a 'dynamic capabilities' approach, to emphasise that the building of distinctive capabilities is a process, and one which must be carried out over long periods of time.

Capabilities must not be treated as fixed, but as evolving in response to the evolving strategic intent of the organisation.

1.2.1 The debate within strategy

In the learning objectives for this book, the resource-based view as an approach to strategy has been described as complementing that of the industry structure approach presented in Book 3. However, it is important to say that there is a debate going on about this view which is, as yet, unresolved. This debate concerns the question as to whether the resource-based view of strategy is a complement to, or a substitute for, the market positioning view of Michael Porter and others.

If the complementary view is accepted, it implies that some industries are intrinsically more attractive than others and that the resource-based view explains why firms differ *within* an industry. On the other hand, it may be more accurate to say that in dynamic industries and sectors, capabilities are the key source of superior performance and profit, because the competition is so dynamic. This view could mean that either the market positioning view is generally wrong, or that it is applicable only to a particular (more stable?) group of industries and that in other industries the resource-based view is more relevant.

Some of the evidence behind this discussion has already been presented in Book 3 which discusses the relative impact of industry structure and organisations' strategies on performance. The work of Rumelt (1991) and Stopford and Baden-Fuller (1990) may be cited in support of the latter view, that the resource-based view is a powerful alternative in explaining sources of advantage over time. It must be stressed that this is a live debate and that Michael Porter continues to put his case strongly.

1.2.2 Combining resources and capabilities

An important aspect of the resource-based approach to strategy is that in order for a capability to be 'distinctive', it must be hard to imitate. We will explore some of the ways in which this can be achieved later in this book. The point to note now is that in order for a capability to be difficult to imitate, it will usually involve drawing on combinations of resources from any and every part of the organisation. It thus extends strategic thinking into human resource management, financial management, organisational development, R&D and technology development and implementation, and so on. In fact, it is more often the way in which organisations combine their resources in bundles that creates uniqueness, which is what we mean by distinctive capabilities. Many of these combinations are a blend of 'hard' tangible elements (such as buildings, equipment, training manuals) and 'soft' intangible elements (such as how well teams work together, the internal culture or the external image of the organisation) which simply cannot be recreated by another organisation.

Let us take as an example the Italian leisure wear retailer Benetton.

MINI-CASE: BENETTON'S CHAIN OF CAPABILITIES

Benetton designs, manufactures, distributes and retails its ranges of brightly-coloured casual clothes around the world. The Benetton business empire began in 1965 in Ponzano, Italy. It was based on the business ideas of Luciano Benetton, who saw the development potential of the beautiful bright colours and designs of knitwear created by his sister Giuliana. Soon the remaining two Benetton brothers were brought into the business, to be the directors of finance and production. From the beginning the business made use of particular resource advantages that were available to them in their local area. There was a great history of local weaving for the textile industry which had existed for hundreds of years. Textiles were, however, organised on a household ('cottage industry') basis. Labour was therefore not only plentiful and cheap, but highly skilled. They could also be employed on a contracted-out, part-time basis. This set a precedent for Benetton, who utilised this flexible part-time workforce as it grew from a small local firm, to a worldwide multinational company with about 7,000 retail outlets.

Benetton used a similar principle in constructing the retail end of its business. As it expanded the number and geographic coverage of its shops, it did so by means of franchises rather than by owning and running the shops. This allowed Benetton to expand very fast, without the need to provide its own capital to fund expansion. Capital was provided by the selected franchisees. Benetton did insist on very tight management contracts however, which committed the franchisee to selling only Benetton products; to tight guidelines on design, colours and layouts of the stores, and so on. Thus Benetton was able to control, without having to own, sales and distribution. This illustrates a principle to which we will return later in this book, that resources do not have to be owned by an organisation in order for that organisation to use and benefit from those resources.

Two other elements of the way Benetton constructed its growing operations are worthy of special mention: first, its just-in-time dyeing/warehousing and distribution logistics chain, and second, its branding/market positioning and advertising. Benetton's retail stores are usually rather small and have little or no backroom storage space. Most stock is on the shelves for customers to see. By linking retail point-of-sale systems directly to the Italian warehousing system, they are able, for re-ordering, to supply stores direct with the lines and colours that prove most popular each season. To achieve this, Benetton uses a system of dyeing grey garments that are being held in store in central warehousing in Ponzano into the requested popular colour combinations, *after* repeat orders are received from the shops. As a result of this dye-to-order process, Benetton is able to achieve yet another resource benefit: it does not tie up capital or risk losing money on storing unpopular stock items in any fashion season. This also enables it to insist on a 'no returns' ordering policy from the franchisees for the stock delivered to the retail stores, since the retailers can re-order what they see is already selling. This, too, minimises Benetton's risk of having unsold stock returned. By far the more usual arrangement between manufacturers and retailers is 'sale or return'.

Benetton was one of the earliest retailers to realise the benefit of using electronic-point-of-sale (EPOS) systems. Benetton used EPOS both to eliminate the cost of holding inventory and replacing it by real sales information, as well as being able to use the information on sales for decisions about current production. Thus, stock was replaced by data. It helped the company to develop switching costs that tied in suppliers and franchisees and shut out competitors.

All branding, market positioning and advertising activities are determined centrally and controlled by the company. Its adverts and Grand Prix racing sponsorship have proved highly controversial over the years, sometimes resulting in court cases (as has happened in Germany and the USA). Advertising campaigns have included the 'United Colors of Benetton' and the social issues campaign featuring advertisements showing a monk and a nun kissing and a young man in the final stages of dying of Aids. Nevertheless, despite, or perhaps as a result of, such controversy, Benetton has been remarkably successful in its worldwide business expansion. Its brand and its products appeal to a worldwide segment of young fashion-conscious people as trend-setting leisure wear. It has been said that if you are over thirty and feel comfortable in a Benetton store, or are *not* outraged by its adverts, then Benetton is losing the focus of its marketing and market positioning.

The business idea behind Benetton's clothing empire is visible to anybody who walks into one of its shops or wears one of its cotton T-shirts or woollen sweaters. However, despite its apparent simplicity and visibility to potential competitors as well as potential customers, the business is constructed around a set of capabilities which are very hard to copy because they arise from the way Benetton has developed over time, and from the way it has invested in and integrated specific resources such as its dyeing-to-order and its ultra-rapid order delivery systems. These distinctive capabilities may even derive from what the company management itself calls the 'Benetton mentality' – a particular mindset about its business, its products, its customers and its management style, embodied in the extended network of

> personal relationships between the Benetton family, their senior management team and their agents. Benetton may be thought of as the brain controlling the central nervous system of a body which manages an extensive system or network of external companies. Figure 1.1 illustrates Benetton's operating network and the structure of linkages in its business chain.
>
> Benetton has created, gradually, a unique business chain – the linking together of a set of activities which is often called by the term 'value chain' (Porter, 1985 – especially Chapter 2). It is not any one resource, or any one link in Benetton's business chain which is so difficult to imitate (despite the emergence of many imitators) but rather the way it all fits together. These unique, hard-to-imitate bundles of resources which combine to create distinctive capabilities in an organisation, are at the heart of the resource-based perspective.

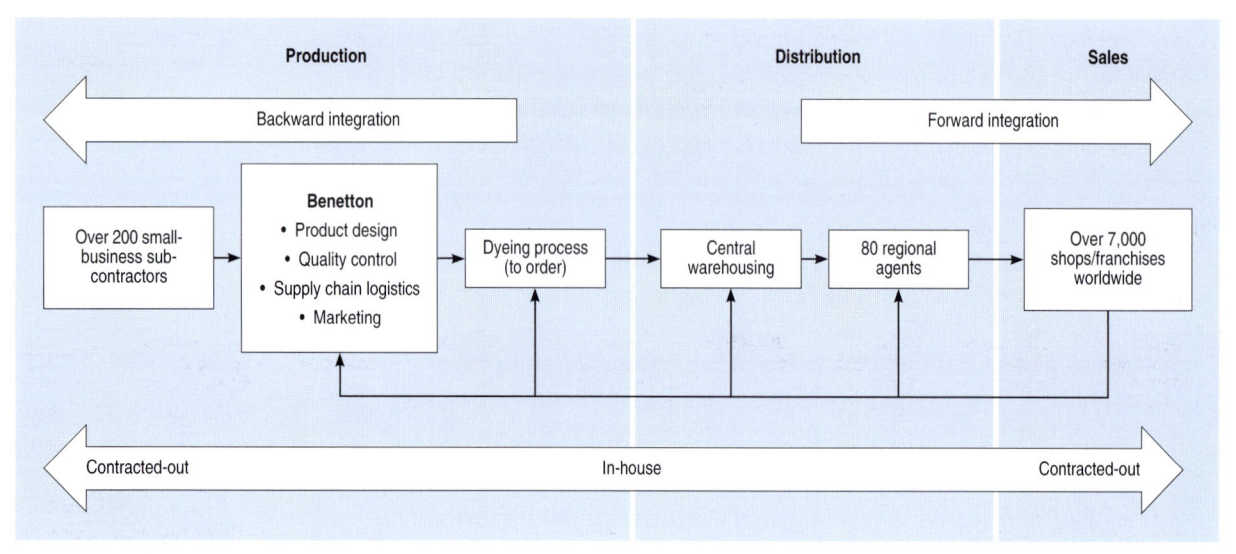

Figure 1.1 Benetton's business chain

Activity 1.1

Having now read some definitions of resources and capabilities together with a mini-case illustrating their meaning in a particular company, you should make a first attempt at listing (a) the resources and (b) the capabilities of your own organisation as you now view them.

1.3 THE VALUE CHAIN CONCEPT AND ITS RELATIONSHIP TO CAPABILITIES

You should now read the following abstracts from the Set Book: pages 118–123 (the sections on 'Identifying capabilities: functions and activities' and 'The architecture of organisational capabilities'). These readings should help you understand more about the value chain.

People often find the concept of a 'value chain' rather difficult to grasp. Let us discuss it further. At its simplest a value chain is an activity path through an organisation. It tells you what it does and the order in which it does it. It should also tell you something about how it does it. A value chain can be a very helpful tool for understanding the difference between two organisations which appear to be functioning in similar ways, in a similar sector. That is because organisations can construct their value chains in very different ways. A different design of the value chain, by which we mean a different activity path through the organisation, might simply indicate different ways of doing things, or it might generate notable sources of increased efficiency.

Value chain

Technology	Product design	Material sourcing	Knitting/cutting process	Assembly	Dyeing (100% internal)	Finishing	Distribution to shops
• Knitting • Cutting • Dyeing	(External)	Wool thread fabrics					

Sources of advantage

• Computerised knitting machines • Computerised cutting turning out 15,000 garments in 8 hours, less than 15% cloth wastage	• Computer transfer of design to knitting or cutting	• Economies of scale in wool thread • Centralised purchasing activities	• Decentralised production • Control of equipment centrally • Total production costs 20% below Europe and Far East manufacturers	• External to take advantage of Italian law • Economies of scale	• Main distinctive product feature under in-house control • Keeps 15–20% of stock 'grey' until colour trends determined • Flexibility	• External • Labour-intensive work kept out of house	• Robotised warehouse • Controlled to allow product to be placed directly on display • Minimises shop inventory

Figure 1.2   Manufacturing value chain for Benetton

Value chain

Design selection by agents	Presentation to shop owners	Order collection by agents	Shopfitting and layout	Receipt of pre-priced merchandise	Advertising	Shop sales and reassortment	Cash collection by central function

Sources of advantage

• Allows field-based experience to determine which designs go into final production	• Agents able to direct shop owners • Agents often part-owners of stores (motivation to succeed)	• Time-consuming process decentralised	• Central control to ensure consistency of image • Shop owners have limited choice but must obtain centrally	• Computer pre-pricing and barcoding • Consistent selling price • Tracking of sales possible • Efficient point-of-sale for customers	• Centrally controlled 'United Colors of Benetton' • Consistent brand image	• System for reallocation of stock between stores to maximise sales • Progress followed by agents and area managers • New window displays every week	• Area managers (Benetton employees) responsible for collection of money

Figure 1.3   Retail value chain for Benetton

Let us return to the example of Benetton discussed above. Figures 1.2 and 1.3 break down into considerably more detail than given in the written text, two related value chains (manufacturing in Figure 1.2 and retail in Figure 1.3) for what Benetton does and how it does it. They clearly illustrate the way in which Benetton has designed its business processes. They further show how this unique construction of their business generates advantage for the company compared with competitor companies seeking to provide similar products and service to the same sort of customers. As a result of its particular value chain, which only means the particular way it has designed its business, Benetton secures specific advantages such as 20 per cent lower production costs than the industry average, and fast response times to actual customer preferences for types of fashion items in their shops.

Value chains can be used to identify sources of increased efficiency and also to facilitate competitive 'benchmarking' of how competitors create value and how their activities compare with yours. Four principles underlie value chain analysis:

1. the size of the cost represented by the activity
2. understanding what factors are driving the costs behind each activity
3. the differing processes of competitor organisations in relation to each activity ('benchmarking')
4. understanding the linkages in the chain and horizontal strategy opportunities.

It could be argued that the last point is the most powerful since it is the total way in which Benetton puts its business activities together that has created a set of distinctive capabilities. However, it is also the way in which they have designed each specific element in the chain to exert control over critical processes in-house. Figure 3.2 later in this book is another value chain, a simple construction to help identify and make sense of the path of activities illustrating how the Novotel hotel chain runs its international hotel business. It summarises each activity (i.e. each link in the chain) and then allows managers to see clearly the linkages *between* each activity, the links that make that particular hotel chain unique.

You may find that even a very simple overview of an organisation's value chain gives a great deal of insight into its relative strengths and weaknesses. It is also the case that imaginative approaches to reconstructing ('reconfiguring') the value chain can release new ways of clustering resources and therefore new types of capabilities within organisations.

Activity 1.2
The chain of capabilities in a school

Following the same logic as the Benetton example, consider what value chain elements may combine to make one primary school better (i.e. more effective) than another? Is it the qualifications of the teachers? The motivation of the children? The pleasantness or otherwise of the location and the facilities?

What you should be looking for in the organisation you select are the bundles of resources which combine together to create distinctive capabilities. How has the organisation used its distinct bundle of assets to achieve superior performance? How does it integrate resources to form capabilities?

Discussion

A different example of the same type of analysis may be to consider the bundle of resources of a city like Barcelona. The mayor and city authorities used the 1992 Olympics to attract massive investment for upgrading new and existing buildings and infrastructure such as railways. This unique opportunity to inject a once-only level of investment also indicates that the mayor had excellent political capabilities. Also required were massive project management capabilities to organise the resources and plan the development processes with a very tight timescale, which often appeared impossible to achieve.

Although you can list many obvious resources that Barcelona (or any town or city) has, such as buildings, scenery, climate, art galleries, shops, regional identity, etc., it is obvious that such a list does not capture the experience of Barcelona as a city. It is the contribution of these specific resources which combine together to create the uniqueness of a particular city. Another city could not reproduce this uniqueness simply by trying to copy one or two buildings. This is another way of understanding what is meant by bundles of resources which combine together to create distinctive capabilities.

2 Why do organisations differ?

We have already explained in the introduction that resources are the source of an organisation's capabilities, whilst capabilities are the main source of its competitive advantage. For this reason, organisations in the same industry are usually heterogeneous (that is, clusters of resources and capabilities are different between organisations) rather than homogeneous (similar between organisations). This does not mean that every organisation within a given sector will be different from every other in that sector. But it does mean that certain organisations within any particular sector will be endowed with resources that enable them to produce more economically and/or better satisfy their customers' needs. This is usually because such resources are in relatively scarce supply and all organisations cannot have equal amounts of them.

For example, some teachers are rated as better than others in teaching skill, experience, subject knowledge, commitment to pupils, etc. Schools differ in their ability to attract and retain such people. Supermarkets may all wish to situate themselves at locations which have good catchment areas of population and good travel connections. But such sites are of limited geographic availability and will be acquired by the larger retail chains who can afford to pay high prices for the land, or who can persuade local government agencies to give them planning and development permission because they are able to promise a given level of investment or jobs in the area.

Therefore, amongst organisations in the same sector, their approach to, and their efficiency at, clustering resources will determine their performance (their level of profitability and their ability to secure and sustain advantage in meeting customer needs). The resource-based approach to strategy assumes such heterogeneity of resources and capabilities between organisations. This has consequences not just in exploiting existing assets specific to individual organisations (organisation-specific or firm-specific assets), but also for the (dynamic) development of new capabilities through learning and capability accumulation. In fact Grant (1991) argues that 'for most firms, the most important capabilities are likely to be those which arise from an integration of individual functional capabilities'. Such strategic capabilities are what Prahalad and Hamel (1990) describe as 'core competences' and what Kay (1993) calls 'distinctive capabilities'.

In general, 'distinctive' capabilities refer to pools of cumulative experience, knowledge and systems that exist within an organisation and that can be used to reduce the cost or time required to create a new resource or extend an existing one.

They include the ability to access, internalise and apply new knowledge. Indeed, this may be regarded as the defining characteristic of a capability-building organisation. This is because resources may diminish in value or relevance over time, yet organisations may be unwilling or unable to develop new ones. Thus, existing sets of resources may become prisons of strategic thinking ('recipes'). Companies can get locked into thinking of their existing resources and capabilities as unique and fail to notice that what was unique has been copied by competitors, so that everybody can do it and the whole sector standard has moved on. Consider the Apple computer company, creators of the Macintosh desktop computer.

> ### MINI-CASE: APPLE COMPUTER INC. AND THE EROSION OF DISTINCTIVENESS
>
> The Apple computer company had a world-beating technology in the 1980s. It was the graphical user interface (GUI) which Xerox PARC had invented but which Apple had brought to the market-place with their Lisa and Macintosh computers. It was the first computer technology using a 'mouse' to control the screen and manage the interface between the user and the machine. It was the first 'user-friendly' personal computer, a computer for people who were nervous using computers. It used pictures, i.e. graphics ('icons'), to represent documents and applications on the computer screen. The icons replaced complex formulas and codes for inputting or accessing software, text or data. This massive technological change created a devoted and loyal group of grateful customers. It was also the basis for the classic differentiation strategy which Apple pursued. It was able to charge a premium price for a genuinely unique offering.
>
> However, competitors gradually caught up with its unique technology, thus eroding the basis of its competitive strategy. It was extremely difficult for Apple to see the extent of the erosion of its distinctive capability and adjust its strategy accordingly in time for it to make a difference. Apple at one point was involved in a long and expensive lawsuit with Microsoft, its largest and toughest competitor. Apple accused Microsoft of stealing its technology and using it as the basis of Microsoft's world-beating Windows software. The case was about intellectual copyright and Apple lost. Apple has gradually and continuously lost market share to rivals who have caught up with its technological advantage and competed away its ability to charge prices well above the industry average. The company is at the time of writing a target for takeover.
>
> To be fair to Apple however, despite the loss of GUI uniqueness, its capabilities in user-friendly software, interfaces, and multimedia, as well as its ability to collaborate with and internalise technology from the world's leading-edge companies, still make the company attractive to predators.
>
> This theme of the evolution of industry structure and its impact on industry dynamics and competitive strategy has been discussed at some length in Book 3.

2.1 RESOURCES AND CAPABILITIES AS SOURCES OF ADVANTAGE

Now read the article by Grant in the Course Reader, 'The resource-based theory of competitive advantage'. Note in particular the definitions of the concepts of 'resources' and 'capabilities' that have already been referred to at the start of this book.

Reflection

Think about Grant's arguments about why the resource-based view in strategy, with its focus on the elements *internal* to the organisation, gives an additional perspective to strategic thinking, complementing that provided by looking mainly at the external environment.

Why does he emphasise organisational processes and organisational routines as important parts of capabilities? Try to think of one or two examples that he gives of capabilities that require processes of co-operation within the organisation in order for the capability to be achieved (e.g. Disney's 'imagineering').

Activity 2.1

Identifying resources

Turn now to Chapter 5 in the Set Book. Look at Figure 5.3 on p. 113. In the 'Resources' box Grant has divided resources up into three separate types: tangible, intangible and human. He also indicates some examples of each type.

Think of a court of law in your own country and try to identify some of the tangible, intangible and human resources which combine to allow it to function.

Now repeat the process of identification for your own organisation.

Then repeat the exercise for your own department.

Discussion

An example from the UK judicial system would be the very old-fashioned (anachronistic?) dress code for barristers and judges who still wear artificial wigs in court. These wigs and the dress robes are tangible, yet they also contribute to some intangibles such as the sense of formality in court proceedings and the idea of 'the dignity of the judge's bench'. These things are therefore both formal and informal symbols. They contribute to attitudes, behaviour and role expectations. They combine all three of Grant's categories: human resources (the lawyers); tangibles (layout of the Court room and the dress robes and wigs); intangibles (reinforcement of the dignity and power of the law by symbols and ceremonial).

You should now watch Video 1 (VC0864) Band 1, 'The Passion for Distinctiveness', in which Robert Grant explores some of his ideas on resources and capabilities and illustrates them in three organisations.

2.2 CONCEPTUAL ANALYSIS OF THE SOURCES OF ADVANTAGE

Organisations differ in their ability to secure advantage from resources and capabilities. That is the basic premise of this book and the underlying assumption of the resource-based view of strategy.

If you are especially interested in the concepts of resources and capabilities, you may now read the article by Amit and Schoemaker, 'Strategic assets and organisational rent', in the Course Reader. This is optional.

Echoing the Reader chapter by Grant, Amit and Schoemaker distinguish between resources and capabilities. They see capabilities as being 'developed over time through complex interactions among the firm's resources'. Amit and Schoemaker argue that *uncertainty, complexity and conflict*, both inside and outside the organisation, *constitute the normal conditions under which managers have to manage*. However, this leaves room for 'discretionary managerial decisions on strategy crafting'. In other words, it is precisely such uncertainties that create the opportunity for heterogeneity between organisations to develop, often as a result of better or worse decision-making by managers about the external environment or the internal resource mix. The article suggests that the challenge facing managers is to identify a set of 'strategic assets' directly arising from the organisation's resources and capabilities. These will be developed as the basis for creating and protecting their organisation's sustainable sources of advantage. The basic idea then inherent in the whole resource-based view of the organisation is to gather and nurture a set of complementary and specialised resources and capabilities which have the following characteristics:

> they should be scarce, durable, not easily traded and difficult to imitate, thus enabling the organisation to secure a revenue stream from them over time and generate superior economic returns from superior performance.

This important set of points about what makes certain resources and capabilities valuable is worth emphasising. Resources and capabilities which are common, short-lived and easy to imitate must be less valuable to an organisation than those which are scarce, durable and difficult to imitate. Rare and inimitable resources and capabilities form the basis of sustainable competitive advantage in strategy.

MINI-CASE: GUIDE DOGS FOR THE BLIND – RARE, INIMITABLE AND NON-SUBSTITUTABLE RESOURCES

A specialised but interesting example of a capability which is hard to imitate and rare, and results in above-average economic returns to the organisation, is the British charity which raises funds for buying, training and supplying guide dogs for the blind. There is a larger British charity which serves the wider needs of the blind, called the Royal National Institute for the Blind (RNIB). The relative success of Guide Dogs for the Blind is explained by the fact that they have large funds which they cannot spend because they are legally only permitted to spend them on activities relating to guide dogs. This customer segment is now almost saturated. Yet the public continues to support it heavily, more heavily than the RNIB which exists to provide for *all* needs of the blind. One explanation for the popularity of Guide Dogs for the Blind with donors is the psychological appeal of the dogs themselves to the general public. This 'appeal' is an intangible resource. It certainly meets the criteria of being scarce, durable and difficult to imitate, and hence valuable. It may outweigh the appeal of the blind themselves who are the recipients for both charities.

A rare, inimitable and non-substitutable resource cluster (see p. 17)

2.2.1 Resources and superior performance

The idea of 'distinctive' competences or capabilities has been around for a long time. Hofer and Schendel (1978) defined them as 'unique resource deployments' (p. 151) which support the organisation's ability to sustain its performance in its existing industries and sectors, or to support it making good in a new sector it is considering entering. The chapter by Amit and Schoemaker in the Reader should be particularly helpful to you in turning resources and capabilities from a set of conceptual elements to ways in which an organisation may begin to put them into operation.

Taking these points further, Peteraf (1993) suggests that although all resources and capabilities have the potential to contribute to superior performance, 'superior resources remain *limited* in supply'. That is why they are rare and valuable (like Apple's GUI or the emotional symbolism of guide dogs) even though their rarity value may not last forever. Figure 2.1 provides a summary of all the factors which affect both the accumulation and limitation of superior resources available to firms in

Peteraf's view. She calls these the 'cornerstones' of competitive advantage. These 'cornerstones' are the key to a firm's ability to earn revenue in excess of break-even from resources (what economists call 'rents').

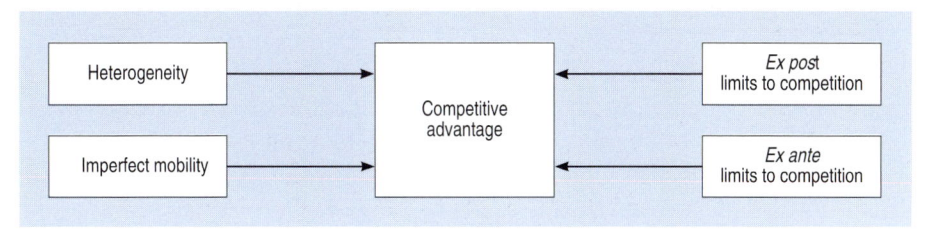

Figure 2.1   Peteraf's 'cornerstones' of competitive advantage (Peteraf, 1993)

Peteraf is concerned with superior performance. Amit and Schoemaker (1993), Barney (1991) and Grant (1991) all agree that what makes superior performance is superior resources and distinctive capabilities. What makes capabilities distinctive is that they must be rare, durable, not easily substituted and not easily traded. The four 'cornerstones' of Peteraf's model explain each of these four conditions.

Taking the four 'cornerstones' of her model in turn, let us begin with '*heterogeneity*'. We have already defined heterogeneity at the start of Section 2. It means that clusters of resources and capabilities are different between firms in the same industry. Organisations with superior resources will be able to produce more economically or better satisfy customer needs. Resources may be unevenly distributed because they are in limited supply: remember the earlier examples of experienced teachers or good supermarket sites. Limited numbers of experienced teachers can be expanded, but only slowly, so many schools have to make do with less experienced teachers and are therefore less likely to satisfy customer needs so well for a considerable time. The case of the number of supermarket sites in good population catchment areas is different. It is a more fixed resource pool which, once saturated, cannot be enlarged. Thus, what is critical is that superior resources remain limited in supply, either permanently or for long periods. It is this which makes them *rare*.

The second cornerstone identified by Peteraf is what she calls 'ex post *limits to competition*'. (The term 'ex post' means something which was not only expected in the light of earlier data, but which has actually happened.) Therefore 'sustained competitive advantage requires that the condition of heterogeneity be preserved'. So if resources are rare for only very short periods of time then the differences between firms will also be very short-lived. What conditions help to preserve rarity? *In order for resources to be durable they must be hard to imitate and difficult to substitute*. This takes us back to our earlier discussion about Benetton and the advantages arising from the way it has linked together its resources into combinations which are hard for competitors to reproduce. This is what is meant by the concept of *causal ambiguity* (Lippman and Rumelt, 1982), where potential imitators do not know exactly what to imitate. In particular, capabilities which develop and accumulate within an organisation from the interconnectedness of the resources which contribute to them, will be particularly hard to imitate. These are capabilities which have a large tacit dimension and are socially complex. They rely on complex processes of organisational learning, which are themselves contingent upon earlier stages and levels of learning, investment and development. They have followed certain pathways of development to arrive at the complex resource bundle they now possess. (This is sometimes called a 'time-path dependency'.)

That is what is meant when we say that certain companies have a research orientation or culture. One of the strongest criticisms used against the conglomerate Hanson when it made a hostile takeover bid against ICI was the claim that Hanson had no experience or appropriate skills to manage a high-value, research-based and knowledge-driven business. The criticism stuck. Their bid failed. Subsequently, in 1993, ICI followed the logic of its own argument and demerged itself into two separate businesses: ICI, which retained the low-value, volume-driven chemicals and aggregates business; and Zeneca, which focused on the high-value, research-driven pharmaceuticals business. This was the conclusion of the view that these two represented fundamentally different businesses, dependent on fundamentally different resources and capabilities which needed managing in different ways.

The third cornerstone is 'ex ante *limits to competition*', that is a limit to the number of organisations competing for a resource. (The term 'ex ante' is a description of a future event which has been extrapolated from present data.) Not all organisations are equally able or willing to bid for a resource, or invest in building a capability. For some organisations the costs (of all kinds, not just financial costs) of implementing particular strategies may be too high, or the outcome too uncertain. This factor means that only a limited number of firms at any one time in any industry are likely to be competing to acquire or build superior resources.

Finally, the fourth cornerstone is that of *imperfect mobility* – that a resource be *not easily traded*. This may take many forms. A resource may be tradable, but be more valuable within the current organisation than elsewhere. A football player who is a star with one team and a particular set of team-mates may never perform as well at another club. Other resources are not tradable because they only have relevance to a specific organisation. Highly productive and experienced coal-miners find their skills to be non-tradable, with little value in any other context.

Another source of limited mobility is what Teece (1982) calls '*co-specialised assets*'. These are specialised resources which are not productive separate from the firm, but must be combined to create value. Consider as an example of this a specialist in particle physics who can only conduct further research with equipment that costs millions of dollars to provide, and technical design and build expertise. Only three or four laboratories in the world provide such conditions. Alternatively, think of rich oil and mineral deposits in the deep parts of the oceans or under the polar ice caps. These mineral resources can only be accessed if combined with highly specialised and expensive equipment, often specially designed for that specific project and requiring immense technical knowledge to use properly. Because immobile resources are not easily traded, their value is likely to stay with the current organisation in the long term.

Peteraf's cornerstones model is saying that heterogeneity in an industry is a fundamental condition for competitive advantage. Indeed, heterogeneity is a fundamental concept of strategy. However, heterogeneity is a necessary, but not a sufficient, condition for sources of advantage to be sustainable. Without the other three cornerstones as well, organisations may have short-lived and easily imitated advantages, which are not sustainable.

Reflection

What do you think of Peteraf's analysis? Has it furthered your understanding of the resource-based approach to strategy?

The model shows how long-term differences in performance cannot be explained by differences in industry conditions. Such an explanation must include an understanding of the contribution of the internal resources of the organisation (the resource-based view). Further, using internal resources productively depends upon organisational and managerial capability.

Peteraf applies her ideas to both single-business strategy and multi-business corporate strategy to show some of the implications for managers of resource-based strategy. At the single-business level her analysis may help managers distinguish between resources which form the basis of a potential advantage and therefore attract investment and other resources which do not. Clarity about imitability of key resources which the organisation possesses should help decide whether and for how long a resource can be protected. This, in turn, should influence the decision on, for example, how rapidly to license out an innovation. An analysis of the quality of resources an organisation possesses should help managers use available resources more effectively and have a better idea of the purposes for which they will be used. Resources which are time-path dependent or which require organisation-specific or firm-specific co-specialised assets are difficult to create or reproduce, but since they cannot easily be imitated they are worth further investment and nurturing.

The resource-based model also lends itself naturally to important issues in corporate strategy concerning the boundaries of the organisation, as we shall see in Section 4 and Book 10.

The next sub-section considers some of the special issues affecting intangible and human resources.

2.3 THE ROLE OF KNOW-HOW, TACIT KNOWLEDGE AND HUMAN RESOURCES

Although it is said so often that it sounds rather trite, people are indeed often the embodiment of distinctive capabilities. It is useful, therefore, to explore the balance of power between the individual and the organisation. In certain types of organisation this is particularly true. For example, in professional service firms the staff are frequently described as 'assets walking around on two legs' because the knowledge and competence of the professional staff, and the trust the client places in that professional competence, are the whole worth of the firm. Without them and their positive commitment, there is minimum value in the business. So consider what happens if professional staff leave. There is a high risk that their clients will leave with them, since often the client trusts the individual, not the organisation. That is because a specific individual (or team) will work with the client over time and become the repository of knowledge concerning that client organisation. That close level of knowledge and contact is itself a person-based competence available to the professional service firm.

MINI-CASE: SAATCHI & SAATCHI'S HUMAN RESOURCES AND ORGANISATIONAL CAPABILITIES

In 1969, two brothers established a small advertising agency in London. From 1975 onwards, by a series of aggressive and spectacular acquisitions, the company expanded rapidly so that by 1987 it had become the biggest advertising agency in the world. Its success was such that in that period it managed to tilt the centre of gravity of the advertising world from Madison Avenue, New York, USA, to Charlotte Street, London, UK. It set a trend which has continued in the advertising industry, for companies to build worldwide networks of agency offices to be able to provide global advertising services to multinational customers.

Saatchi & Saatchi made a bid for world market leadership in their sector. The strategy was to provide global business services for global corporations and to position the agency as a brand for quality services worldwide. The rationale was to match the global expansion of their multinational clients. They saw an increase in the proportion of advertising turnover being handled by international agencies. They argued that use of a single agency by clients would be seen as commitment to global marketing and more centralised control of campaigns and international market positioning. It also offered greater consistency. The increasing availability of global media (international newspapers and journals, satellite broadcasting) made this approach more feasible than previously.

In some areas they were highly effective in getting the benefit from economies of scale. Some examples of this would include ruthless exploitation of economies of scale in media-buying (i.e. negotiating bulk discounts for television and radio time or pages of space in newspapers, magazines or billboards) and an ability to attract and retain high-quality 'creative' staff. However, they were less effective at putting other key parts of the strategy into operation, especially those aspects of central financial control that were essential to securing the major benefits from expansion, such as lower costs and operational efficiencies; or cross-selling of complementary services, such as public relations advice. In fact, any tight central financial and strategic control virtually disappeared when their financial director Martin Sorrell left to start building his own rival chain of agencies. This became WPP, the owner of the J. Walter Thomson and Ogilvy and Mather agencies.

The Saatchi brothers, Maurice (left) and Charles (right)

Increasingly, cash from the core business was invested in further supposedly 'related' acquisitions such as public relations, corporate identity, market research, direct marketing, sales promotion, management consultancy and legal services firms. These were further and further away from their advertising agency roots. Nevertheless, for a long time the shares remained highly rated and the Saatchis attained almost 'guru' status in preaching the gospel of service conglomerates (i.e. 'one-stop shopping' for a whole range of business and professional services to be provided by the same supplier).

This came to an abrupt halt in 1987 when they made a bid to buy a British bank. The bid was for Midland Bank, later bought by the Hong Kong and Shanghai Banking Corporation (HSBC). Saatchi & Saatchi's bid for Midland Bank was greeted with complete incredulity and the share price collapsed, putting the whole company into a cash crisis. It became increasingly difficult for them to service their interest payments on borrowings which had financed their acquisitions. In 1989 a new French chief executive was brought in. He had a reputation for tough financial management. Costs were gradually brought under control. Meanwhile, Saatchis' client base and revenue had always remained strong since the agency was well-regarded in its core business. A large number of blue chip clients remained extremely loyal to the agency and to the Saatchi brothers in particular. Charles Saatchi was widely regarded in the industry as an advertising genius and was revered by many clients.

The issue of the share price remained unresolved. Some powerful shareholders never forgave the Saatchi brothers for what they regarded as their irresponsible mismanagement of the firm. Matters finally came to a head in 1994, triggered by an American corporate investor who secured enough votes on the Saatchi board to get Maurice Saatchi ousted as chairman.

This public humiliation of Maurice Saatchi, sacked as chairman of the advertising agency he co-founded with his brother 25 years earlier, led to a rapid resignation of both Saatchi brothers accompanied by many other senior staff loyal to the founders. This was accompanied by the equally humiliating loss of a number of high-profile and valuable client accounts, such as Mars and British Airways. The contracts of employment which attempted to tie professional staff to the agency, and prevent them joining their old boss in his new agency, were virtually unenforceable. Many of Maurice Saatchi's closest colleagues rapidly found their way to the new rival agency M. and C. Saatchi (known as 'New Saatchi'). It has traded very successfully since its inception. 'Old' Saatchi has meanwhile changed its name to Cordiant and sought to attract new business to make up for the lost accounts.

Activity 2.2

Consider the pattern of events affecting Saatchi & Saatchi's human resources and organisational capabilities, just described in the mini-case. Try to think of other examples in similar professional service organisations.

Consider your own organisation. Can you identify some examples of 'know-how' embodied in particular individuals or teams? What would be the effect in the organisation if these individuals or teams left? How could the organisation rebuild or replace the 'know-how' they represent?

2.3.1 Tacit knowledge

The same pattern as described in the Saatchi & Saatchi mini-case can be seen happening in financial services. For example, in investment banks or corporate finance houses key teams often leave (or are poached by rivals) *en masse*. This represents a total loss of expertise in that area (for example the analyst team for a particular industry). One of the consequences of this is that acquisitions in professional services, whether it be an advertising agency, an investment bank, a consultancy practice or a software house, are inherently high-risk. That is because what you are acquiring is the knowledge and expertise of the staff, who represent around 80 per cent of the value of the business and who may leave, taking their expertise with them. In addition, most of this is *tacit* knowledge (Polyani, 1966) which is not easily codified and stored permanently with the organisation.

Tacit knowledge is usually defined as that which cannot be written down or specified. It is embedded in the interactive routines, rituals and behaviours of individuals within their organisations. Many now argue that knowledge, particularly tacit knowledge, is strategically the most significant resource of the organisation (Quinn, 1992; Grant, 1991). That is because tacit knowledge in particular demonstrates one of the most valuable characteristics for resource-based sources of competitive advantage – it is almost impossible for rivals to imitate or replicate.

Knowledge is largely an intangible resource and as such is more difficult to imitate than tangible resources such as buildings or machinery. Nonaka (1991) argues that tacit knowledge has a cognitive dimension in that it consists of mental models that individuals follow in given situations. These mental models are internal processes of sense-making and decision-making and may be personal to an individual or shared by members of a team or a department. We use such mental models all the time in our daily life. Think for example of what makes a good doubles team playing tennis. It is the mutual anticipation of play and moves by the two partners. That suggests some of the reasons why resources of this type are extremely hard to imitate and hence particularly valuable. One of the strongest reasons for the high value and low imitability of tacit knowledge is that it illustrates once again the concept of 'causal ambiguity': uncertainty regarding the causes of effectiveness in organisations. Often the organisation itself does not fully know the precise nature of its source of advantage. This, too, makes the resource impossible to imitate and inherently sustainable.

To consider this point further, reflect back on the description of the cumulative sources of advantage of Benetton discussed earlier in Section 1.3. Rumelt (1984) calls these types of resources 'isolating mechanisms', in that they protect sources of advantage by restricting competition.

Some professional service firms (such as the US accounting and consulting firm Arthur Andersen) go to great lengths to develop internal systems and procedures for storing and reproducing and making explicit such implicit knowledge. They attempt to replicate and thereby standardise and routinise as many organisational procedures as possible. Their manuals are updated continually to disseminate best practice firm-wide. Their content covers every aspect of professional work, such as how to approach a potential client, or how to bid for an assignment. Utilisation of these procedural manuals is mandatory throughout the firm.

Although such manuals are an attempt to capture and codify tacit knowledge, what they actually capture is what Nonaka (1991) calls 'explicit knowledge' or objective knowledge. That is knowledge which can be shared so that at the end of the knowledge communication the recipient knows as much as the provider. This is never the case with tacit knowledge, which contains experience, skills (Nelson and Winter, 1982) and know-how.

Whilst Chandler (1962) championed the view of the top-down hand of management controlling systems and procedures, Nonaka (1991) argues for the middle-up view of management, emphasising the critical role of middle managers in knowledge creation and knowledge capture. To quote Nonaka (p. 104):

> Middle managers synthesised the tacit knowledge of both frontline employees and senior executives, made it explicit, and incorporated it into new technologies and products. In this respect, they are the true 'knowledge engineers' of the knowledge-creating company.

Having discussed some resources with very special characteristics, we can move on in the next section to look at the broader context in which resources have to be relevant, effective and appropriate, both for the strategic intent of the organisation and for the changing characteristics of the industry or sector.

3 Resources and capabilities

In the nineteenth century and earlier, most factors of production were immobile across frontiers; differentiated, branded products were very rare; and traders dealing in commodity products were the norm. Most resources were therefore tied to a specific geographic location. By the second half of the twentieth century, different factors of production which were mobile and not location-specific had become critical. Table 3.1 shows some of the differences.

Table 3.1 Old and new critical resource endowments	
Old immobile resources	**New mobile resources**
• land	• technology
• labour	• information
• capital	• brands
	• open international financial markets

As Table 3.1 shows, the old immobile assets and resources have been replaced by more permeable mobile ones. Land is obviously location-specific. Organisations derived advantage from manufacturing or producing at a given location because of that location's particular feature, such as access to roads or ports or especially fertile soil or a raw material. Labour also used to be tied to location and provided special local skills or low-cost labour.

Financial markets then were not global, or even very international, and much capital available was local capital ploughed back into local businesses. Financial capital markets are now fluid, transparent and global, so that even the 'old' resources are now no longer immobile. The new key resources are much more transferable across nations and markets and many are intangible rather than tangible. Many of these resources may be successfully located almost anywhere, as long as the organisation is able to secure its access to them.

From the middle of the nineteenth century onwards, the phenomenon of labour migration from rural to urban areas or across different parts of the globe, has been continuing. In addition, modern communication technologies have made many aspects of specialised labour available and accessible without physically moving people to the same location. Hence the dramatic rise in software companies in India, where skilled programmers are available to multinational companies at a fraction of the salary levels in Europe, Japan or North America. Not only is this a plentiful and cheap pool of highly-skilled labour, there is also a further advantage – staff living within a complementary time zone. That means that the Indian workforce working during the day can effectively process data for a European company overnight. In the same way, 'telemedicine' allows doctors based in Austin or Muscat to diagnose patients' illnesses in the remote deserts of West Texas and South Oman, respectively.

Resources can be located anywhere in the world and the new types of critical resources (such as finance or information) are very mobile indeed. An important organisational capability, then, is that the organisation be able to effectively manage its resources, whatever their location.

3.1 THE ECONOMICS OF STRATEGY: MARKETS OR HIERARCHIES

'A study in the economics of internal organisation' is the subtitle Oliver Williamson (1975) gave to his original study *Markets and Hierarchies*, in which he used the transaction cost approach as the basis for deciding the shape, size and optimal boundaries of an organisation. The argument is a simple one. Transaction cost economics suggests that the most efficient way to carry out a transaction is whichever way will minimise the costs of that transaction to the organisation. Such costs may include the setting up and running of a contract, internal costs of management time and resource, costs of operating at less than optimal scale efficiency, and so on. The idea is that the level of the costs of the transaction will determine whether it is most appropriately carried out internally within the organisation itself (within the organisational hierarchy) or in markets (buy the product, component or service in from outside). When making these calculations it is the total cost over the lifetime of the transaction which is the relevant comparison to make with the cost of keeping the transaction in-house.

This may appear rather a laboured academic argument. However, we have become completely accustomed to it as the practice of 'contracting out' facilities, functions or services to the most efficient provider. This is now commonplace within both the public and the commercial sectors in most developed economies. It is being popularised worldwide as part of the process of privatisation of the state sector. Transaction costs were the theoretical underpinning for looking at the provision of services by both local and national government on the basis of the most efficient use of resources and the lowest costs of the transaction. Should local government employ its own street cleaners? Should schools and hospitals provide their own catering? Should national agencies build and operate power generation and transmission facilities? Or should these services be bought in from outside contractors which specialise in them and can therefore pass on both their expertise and their greater potential scale economies to their customers?

Similar arguments have been explored in private companies also. They encompass not only cleaning, catering and security services, but also entire functions such as provision and maintenance of computer systems, routine data processing functions such as payroll, and even strategically important information systems. These decisions have formed the basis of massive growth in new business services companies such as EDS (Electronic Data Systems) whose phenomenal business growth since 1980 is largely due to the explosion in demand for facilities management. On this basis the entire computing and IS (information systems) functions of an organisation (whether public, like tax collection agencies, or commercial, like airlines) is carried out by EDS for the client. As part of this reallocation of resources, EDS and other similar firms usually take the staff from the client company who had previously performed that function internally onto their own payroll. Similarly, BP has its entire accounting function and systems run by Andersen Consulting. Organisations need to be clear about the strategic significance of such decisions on the overall balance of their resources and capabilities, both current and future.

Transaction cost economics is central to a discussion of strategy as competing through capabilities. What it means is that transaction decisions determine the shape, size and resource base of the organisation. It contributes to answering these fundamental questions:

- What is important that we do internally to secure our customers and markets?
- For which parts of what we do is it better to carry out activities outside our boundaries and buy in?

The answers to these kinds of 'make or buy' question have transformed the size and boundaries of schools, hospitals, local government departments and prisons, as well as companies. Table 3.2 summarises the conditions under which either hierarchies (internal markets) or external markets are preferred.

Table 3.2 Hierarchies or markets?

For hierarchies if:	For markets if:
• economies of scale, scope or learning	• commodity products
• fewer opportunistic actions	• where market mechanism needed
• in thin markets (with few choices)	• profit maximisation and motivation important
• in complex uncertain asset-specific situations	• entrepreneurship necessary
• where information is uneven	• bureaucratic difficulties and/or high governance costs
• risk of information leakage	• routine situations
• strategic capabilities	

The whole issue of markets or hierarchies concerns choices organisations make about how and where to do things. It provides us with a way of understanding some of the reasoning behind the different ways that organisations construct their value chains. It is also central to the issue addressed in Section 4 of this book: the boundaries of the organisation. Let us elaborate on one or two of the factors listed in Table 3.2 to see why.

An obvious point on which to begin is that of doing something in-house if there is *risk of information leakage*. (You may remember this as an issue in the SATRA worked case study.) For example, should EDS take over all IT and IS functions for the police, or is criminal information too sensitive to out-source even if the data-capture and data-processing function could be handled more efficiently? Should commercial printing firms be allowed to print the official publications of procedure and debate in the European Parliament?

The condition of '*fewer opportunistic actions*' means that keeping a resource in-house will affect management behaviour regarding that resource. It may encourage a longer-term view on development of its possible uses. It may encourage more imaginative uses, perhaps in collaboration with other resources. This may affect, for example, organisational decisions about investing in training or professional and personal development. That is not to say that external suppliers do not train their staff. It is more that the nature of the training may be designed for their objectives rather than yours.

Consider a different example. Computer reservations systems are the central nervous systems of the modern international travel industry. They are the means by which airlines, hotels, car hire companies, etc. manage reservations and ticketing services to customers and between themselves. They are also an invaluable source of market data about customers for marketing purposes. However, they are extremely expensive to set up and maintain. Only one airline owns its own system: American Airlines has its Sabre network. All other airlines either share jointly owned systems such as Amadeus or Galileo, or buy transactions from competitor airlines' shared systems. This represents a cost to them and a revenue stream to the rival airline. When the Scandinavian airline SAS was forced for reasons of cost to leave full membership of the Amadeus computer reservation system of which it had been a founder member, it did not lose access to the system. It could access the system by paying on a transaction-by-transaction basis. What it lost was the ability to influence the future design and development of the system to suit SAS business needs. It also lost access to the database that Amadeus represented.

Activity 3.1

Transaction costs and capabilities

Following that general discussion of the 'make or buy' decision for organisations, it is important to think about the consequences of that decision for the capabilities of the organisation – present and future.

- What, if any, activities has your organisation contracted out in recent years?
- What, if any, effect has this had, intended or unintended, on the types of work that other departments in the organisation have been able (or unable) to carry out?
- What does this tell you about the way that resources contribute to capabilities?
- If your organisation has had no contracting out, then for the purposes of this Activity, you should try to identify possible functions or areas in your organisation where this might be feasible. Then you should carefully analyse the impact of any such moves on the rest of the organisation and its existing resources and capabilities. Possible areas of contracting that you might consider have been given in the text. Common ones are: catering, cleaning, payroll, security, training, etc.

Discussion

This activity should have made you more aware of the practical relationship between resources and capabilities. Every organisation should be able to distinguish between activities which it regards as core activities and those which it regards as peripheral. Much of the time people do not think about the difference between core and peripheral activities until they have to. The reason may be a change in government policy towards funding (e.g. for schools, local government authorities, etc.) or competition from a lower-cost competitor (e.g. telephone-banking companies such as First Direct offering all banking services to customers over a telephone line without the need to buy and maintain buildings, as required for traditional high street bank branches). Whatever the cause, the effect is to make necessary a review of what the organisation does, why and how. This in turn requires an understanding of its current use of resources and whether those resources are essential to a core capability.

For example, is it essential to education and learning in a school that only fully-qualified teachers carry out supervision of children at breaks and mealtimes? Is it perfectly adequate for medical auxiliaries to set simple bone fractures in accident and emergency departments of busy hospitals? The answers to these questions will vary according to what each organisation judges to be core or peripheral to objectives and customer needs. It may also provide a basis for differentiating between one type of service provider and another within the same market.

A further point to note is that designating a resource 'peripheral' is not always the end of the matter. It may not be quite so clear-cut. Not all organisations feel able or willing to contract-out their IS function or their bone-setting. That may be because on analysing the situation they realise that the data gathered and processed within their IS function is highly valuable market data about their customers, which they would do better to gather and process themselves. (This is what Table 3.2 means by a strategic capability.*) Even more critical are management information systems which gather information from across all business functions to provide managers with the information they need to understand their organisation. Equally, a hospital may find that the ability of a medical auxiliary to judge when a fracture is indeed 'simple' or not causes too many problems and results in expensive litigation from patients.*

We will return to these issues in Section 4 when we look in more detail at the boundaries of the organisation.

3.2 THE ECONOMICS OF MULTI-PRODUCT OR MULTI-BUSINESS ORGANISATIONS

Your answers to Activity 3.1 should help you to understand what is meant by 'economies of scope' (Teece, 1980, 1982) and 'synergy'. Economies of scope are economies derived from integration, from using the same resource more intensively. This means that resources acquired for one purpose can be used for another purpose at little or no extra cost. Technically, that is what synergy should mean in practice. Any organisation talking about obtaining synergies from various parts of its operations should be able to point directly to the sources of economies of scope that will deliver those synergies. Teece calls these 'complementary assets'.

Consider the following example. The charge card company American Express is able to offer a free travel arrangement service to its gold and platinum card-holders. It will make all enquiries as to mode, style and time of travel and recommend best options. It will then book all travel arrangements and reservations for the client. In order to provide this free service to the customer it makes use of the international information processing, transaction and distribution systems that it has already built up to carry out its main blue card business. These are already connected into a worldwide network of airline reservation systems, hotel reservation systems, car hire chains, theatre booking services, etc. All American Express has to do to provide the additional dedicated travel service to its most valued group of customers is to provide a small number of dedicated staff who will tap into the existing network. That is an economy of scope.

Similarly, schools may get economies of scope from having specialist teachers in particular subject areas who are able to teach many different levels of courses for many different types of qualification. The resource is the expertise of the teacher. The economy of scope is spreading that expertise across a variety of organisational outputs.

The availability of scope economies may lead organisations to structure themselves in such a way as to secure those benefits if at all possible. Management expertise may be such a scope economy, in that it can be spread across a number of related product areas, markets or sectors.

Many companies which are involved in a number of joint ventures, or strategic alliances covering various parts of their value chain, may be perceived as 'virtual' organisations. Although they are separate organisations, each depends upon the others for performing important parts of its activities. They have so many shared interests and resources, that to regard them as separate entities in anything other than a legal sense would be misleading. Some discussion of shared or distributed resources, networks and 'virtual' organisations is found later in Section 4. Some well-known companies such as Unilever and Royal Dutch Shell have grown in this way historically as part of the development process of arriving at their present structures. It is now becoming more common for such networks to be not just transitional but permanent types of organisational form.

We will return in detail to the topic of strategic alliances in Books 10 and 11.

3.3 GRANT'S FIVE-STAGE MODEL

You should now read Chapter 5 in the Set Book. Skim the chapter if you wish, since you will already have read the article by Grant in the Course Reader which covers some similar ground.

The chapter provides you with an overview of the concepts and strategic issues that have been addressed in this book so far about the resource-based view of the organisation and its relationship to strategic management. As a result of reading this chapter you should appreciate:

- that resources and capabilities internal to the organisation are the main vehicle for achieving superior performance
- that resources and capabilities internal to the organisation should therefore form a basis for strategy formulation as well as for strategy implementation
- that organisations should therefore seek self-knowledge about the strength of their principal resources and capabilities, *relative to competitors*
- that organisations should ensure that their existing resources are fully and effectively used

- that organisations should ensure that they identify and develop future resource needs.

The chapter spends a lot of time classifying different types of resources, which is an essential first step for organisations seeking to understand their own resources. An important point to note is that 'accounting book values usually bear little relationship to the true value of a firm's resources', especially where the most important resources of an organisation are not only intangible, but also invisible. Grant mentions the take-off and landing slots which are essential to an airline being able to function, yet are not owned by the company. A rather different example may be the 'influence' of a chief executive with other influential business or governmental figures. For example, a Lebanese gasoline retailing company continued to supply all areas of Beirut throughout the prolonged 20-year civil war. The company's ability to do this depended entirely on the chief executive's contacts with parties on both sides of the conflict's front lines. This was the key resource contributing to the firm's ongoing success, although the company's accounts placed no formal value on the chief executive's survival.

Having discussed such resource identification and classification issues, Grant moves to their relation to capabilities. As you will remember from the definitions of the distinction between a resource and a capability, resources are only the building blocks for capabilities. Always bear in mind that strategy is concerned with superior performance. Therefore the important strategic issue regarding capabilities is that it is not capabilities *per se* that matter, but capabilities *relative* to other competitor organisations. This is captured in Table 5.3 (p. 120).

Value chain analysis gives a useful starting-point for identifying capabilities and their flow through the organisation, but it still does not adequately reflect the way in which clusters of resources have to work *together* to create capabilities. In this respect Figure 5.7, p. 123, showing a hierarchy of organisational capabilities for a telecommunications equipment manufacturer, should be helpful. It shows that higher-level capabilities require the integration of lower-level capabilities. It also illustrates the point that capabilities can only be integrated by the behaviour and knowledge of people. It is that which makes higher-level capabilities complex and difficult to imitate. For example, new product development is a *process*, not a function. The process relies on *integration* across functions. The same is true of a rugby team practising its line-outs, or a medical team in an operating theatre or accident department of a hospital. Setting up a communications channel or a cross-functional team does not guarantee that they will work effectively. To work effectively the functional knowledge and individual experience that the team contains must be integrated and co-ordinated.

One increasingly common way of helping organisations appraise, develop and improve their capabilities is through 'benchmarking', which encourages comparison with other organisations. Benchmarking against standards or practices of other organisations can encourage rapid improvements. It is a very useful way to encourage individuals, departments and whole organisations to be more realistic about how good they think they are at what they do. Organisations always have a tendency to be inward-looking and self-congratulatory about how well they do what they do. Benchmarking can introduce a more objective perspective, and remind us that it is not capabilities *per se* that matter, but capabilities *relative* to competitors that determine superior performance.

3.3.1 Sustainability and appropriability of returns from resources and capabilities

The factors reviewed in the Set Book affecting sustainability of competitive advantage should be familiar from Section 2.2. The same categories are used: *durability, replicability* (difficult to imitate, 'inimitable') and *mobility* (not easily traded, 'immobile' and 'non-substitutable').

However, the discussion moves on to the further question of '*appropriability*' – who benefits from the resource or capability. It is not always the organisation that owns the resource which benefits from it. Indeed it may benefit more from resources it does not own: think back to the example of the airline and its take-off and landing slots. Appropriability, however, is more specific than that. It refers to the returns generated from a resource. Grant uses three categories to explain this: property rights, relative bargaining power and the embeddedness of the resource.

Property rights over equipment are reasonably straightforward. Patents over inventions and formulas or contracts covering intellectual property are notoriously unclear. Think of the multimillion dollar lawsuit between the pop singer George Michael and Sony, which owned his recording contract. George Michael felt his artistic creativity to be constrained by Sony's management of its music business. He lost the case, but by late 1995 was negotiating his departure to Dreamworks, the new entertainment company set up by Steven Spielberg and others. So what did Sony actually own? It certainly owned all his historic recordings but not the effect of motivation on the quality of his future creativity. This reminds us of the advertising executives of Saatchi & Saatchi. Consider also who owns the 'public service ethos' of local government officers.

In a professional service firm, who 'owns' the expertise of the professional or the good relationship with the client? Contracts for these things are virtually unenforceable. Relative strength of bargaining power resides with the individual. Employment contracts at The Open University clearly spell out ownership of the intellectual output of an academic faculty by the organisation. This does not prevent such faculty from publishing other separate output of books and articles based on the same specialised knowledge. To what extent they are using the organisation's facilities, systems and reputation to help them do so ('embeddedness') is open to interpretation. It is not, however, open to legal enforcement. These examples highlight the lack of clarity affecting implementation for all three of Grant's categories: property rights, relative bargaining power and embeddedness of the resource.

Lastly, the chapter moves from thinking about current to future requirements: the dynamic of replenishing, renewing and adding to the organisation's resources and capabilities.

3.3.2 Putting it all together

Figure 3.1 reproduces the framework from p. 138 of the Set Book: the five-stage model.

The model structures the arguments into a five-stage process which any organisation can use to guide it through the process of analysing resources and capabilities. As you can see this is not a linear model, but a circular, iterative one. Here the loop goes back from stage 5 to stage 1

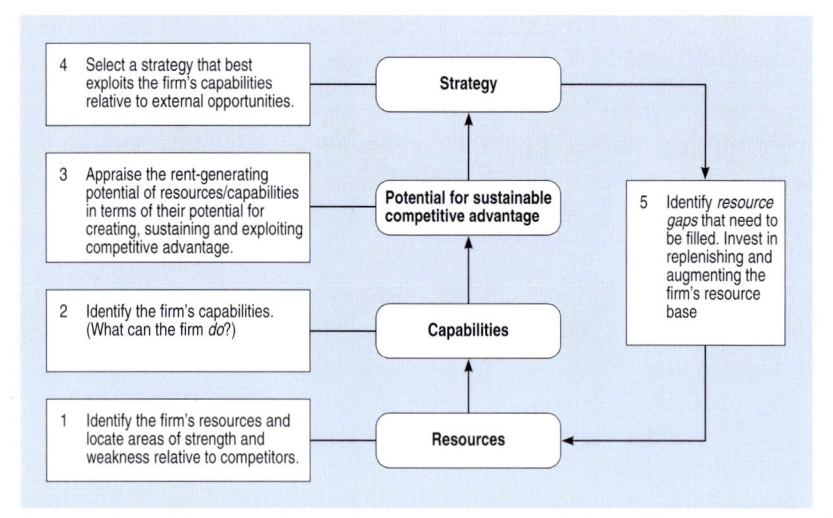

Figure 3.1 A framework for analysing resources and capabilities (Grant, 1995)

every time, in order to emphasise the continuous process of build-up and decay which resources undergo. Resources and capabilities are dynamic, not static. Their relevance and applicability usually have a lifespan governed either by industry structural changes, (as illustrated in the European food-processing industry mini-case in Book 3), or by erosion of distinctiveness (as illustrated by the Apple computer mini-case).

3.3.3 Making it happen

The issue that lies at the heart of the resource-based approach, and which is implicit rather than explicit in Grant's work, is implementation, 'making it happen'. By that is meant the ability to use the resources, structures and routines within the organisation to create capabilities. This ability is itself a capability and perhaps the most critical an organisation possesses: the organisational capability to transform resource potential into dynamic capabilities.

The next sub-section contains a mini-case of a company trying to learn how to do precisely that. However, before moving on, it may be helpful to relate these points back to the analysis you have already carried out on the SATRA Worked Case Study.

Activity 3.2

Return to Figure 3.1 above. Try to relate it to the case analysis carried out for SATRA.

SATRA provides a useful example of all five categories of resources:
- financial (static subscription income; insufficient funds for essential reinvestment and for developing research)
- physical (deteriorating, poorly-maintained buildings with bad inter-linking between them)
- human (demotivated professional staff; poor management/staff relations; poor communications; inappropriate management structure; inadequate staff development)
- technological (need to upgrade computing facilities, both hardware and software, to improve response times to customers; inadequate chemical analysis equipment; poor internal management information systems)

- reputation (status as leading international research centre under threat).

Go through each of the five stages of Figure 3.1 for SATRA. Note the similarities and differences to the Business Planning Framework used by the company in the case.

Discussion

The formulation of the new strategy had to respond to the tougher external environment SATRA faced. However, it also, very importantly, had to reflect the critical internal resources and capabilities of the organisation. In SATRA's case we know that 70 per cent of its current cost was its professional staff, without whose professional expertise it did not have a business. We also know that it was experiencing increasing problems retaining its graduate recruits since it offered them very little in the way of professional or personal development. Its strategic options were therefore circumscribed by this internal resource management requirement, since its key resource (information) was largely 'embedded' in the intellectual creativity and expertise of its professional staff.

To use the language and concepts of this book, SATRA had problems with the sustainability and appropriability of its critical resources and capabilities. Its internal resources and capabilities formed the principal basis for its new strategy formulation as well as for subsequent strategy implementation.

Its revised strategy enabled SATRA to use the resources, structures and routines within the organisation to create new capabilities. This ability is itself an organisational capability which can transform resource potential into dynamic capabilities.

The next section looks at a company trying to learn how to do precisely that on a continuous basis.

3.4 THE ROLE OF ORGANISATIONAL ROUTINES AND LEARNING IN BUILDING AND TRANSFERRING CAPABILITIES

The mini-case which follows analyses the process of long-term capability-building within a successful multinational hotel chain, Novotel (adapted from Segal-Horn, 1995; Baden-Fuller *et al.*, 1995). It looks at the accumulation of core skills through learning mechanisms within the firm. The analysis provides detailed illustration of the internal mechanisms by which capabilities are identified, developed and then transferred across the company's international operations. It examines the organisational structures, processes and routines that it has created to implement its strategy. It provides insight into the role of capabilities in the development of competitive advantage for an international service firm. Service firms are characterised by particular combinations of resources and capabilities different from those characteristic of manufacturing firms, the most obvious difference being the predominance in service organisations of the point of contact between the front-line staff and the customer. The resource-based approach focuses on the creation and sharing of knowledge-based resources and is particularly helpful for service industries, since most services are heavily dependent on knowledge-based resources in both the design and delivery of the service, and especially on the tacit knowledge underpinning the routines of staff.

The assumption fundamental to resource-based strategy suggests that explanations of the competitive advantage of firms within the same industry context may be provided by exploring the internal processes for capability building, capability management and capability retention of different competitors. It also suggests different processes of asset accumulation and asset sustainability by individual firms. The brief discussion of some of Novotel's capability building and capability management processes is an attempt to get inside the detail of what these concepts mean in practice. It also shows how these processes may provide defensible sources of advantage to organisations that have the capability to use them effectively.

The strategic management task for Novotel is to create processes for meeting customer expectations in all its hotels worldwide. It must therefore achieve consistency whilst still enabling all front-line and managerial staff to deal sensitively and helpfully with customer needs.

MINI-CASE OF A MULTINATIONAL HOTEL CHAIN: THE CREATION AND SHARING OF KNOWLEDGE-BASED ASSETS

The first Novotel hotel was opened by two entrepreneurs near Lille airport in France in 1967. The first Novotel outside France was opened in 1973. By 1995 the chain had grown to 280 hotels in 46 countries around the world. The hotels provide 43,000 rooms and employ 33,000 people. Novotel is just one of the hotel chains belonging to the Accor Group of France, which operates more than 2,000 hotels worldwide offering more than two million rooms at different ratings and service levels. Other chains in the group include Sofitel, Mercure, Ibis, Formule 1. These range from 4-star (Sofitel) to 1-star (Formule 1).

The fundamental characteristic of the Novotel hotel concept is the international standardisation of the offering. What is therefore required is consistency of the offering in every location in which it is available. This means putting in place a system that is robust enough to generate consistent service standards to satisfy customer expectations, irrespective of local conditions or infrastructure. Some of the elements of standardisation are easily realisable. The design, style and layouts of the hotels are reproduced to precise specifications. For example, bedroom size is standard throughout Europe at 24 square metres, although this does differ for Novotel Asia. The Novotel chain is positioned as a 3-star chain worldwide, which means that certain facilities such as quality of bedroom furniture, fixtures and fittings or outside amenities such as swimming pools and amounts of free car parking space are always available at all Novotel units.

Figure 3.2 captures some of the key elements in the Novotel business chain. However, the more interesting elements of the Novotel offering for the purposes of this discussion are the management processes which enable the service levels to be delivered at all locations worldwide.

Product design	Marketing	Distribution	Service provision	Service monitoring and enhancement
• Hospitality concept • 3-star • Features • Layout • Locations • Image • Homogeneity • NPD	• Corporate travel management • Partnership programmes • Special promotions • Pricing • Geographic network • Advertising themes • Materials	• Global reservation systems • Networks • Travel agencies	• Purchasing efficiencies • Supplier partnership programmes • Staff multi-skilling • Staff exchanges • Multi-culture	• Customer surveys • Quality measures • Compliance measures • Directors' clubs/progress groups

Figure 3.2 The Novotel business chain (Teare and Armistead, 1995)

Since hotel design and guest bedrooms are standardised, basic housekeeping and maintenance functions can in turn be standardised. That means that the training of staff in all basic functions may be simplified and training procedures themselves standardised. Indeed, one of the features of Novotel's parent company the Accor Group, is the 'Académie Accor', set up in 1985 as the centre for all staff training within the group. Its 'campus' is located on the site of group corporate headquarters just outside Paris. From there, all training is designed and delivered. This standardised approach to the core service concept places special requirements on the staff as the key medium for delivery of consistent service standards wherever the customer is staying. Standardised procedures and centrally designed training programmes are one of the core mechanisms for securing such consistency.

Taking the notion of consistency one stage further, the Novotel senior management developed a new approach to staffing in the hotel sector which is described as 'multi-skilling'. ('Polyvalence' is the correct French word; however, the word 'multicompetence' is frequently used inside Novotel because of its similarity to English words.) The idea behind multi-skilling is to develop staff as a team able to perform all tasks and work as needed in a flexible manner. Obviously, this has many advantages for hotel management, not least in smoothing the need for certain types of staff at peak periods of the day or evening. Pressures on checking-in or checking-out at reception cluster at early morning and evening. This, and getting rooms cleaned while guests are at breakfast, are common bottlenecks dramatically affecting patterns of staffing. With the Novotel approach to flexible skilling and team working, a new pattern emerged. Flexible working patterns broke down the staff demarcation, normal within the rest of the hotel industry. Reception and front-of-house activities (e.g. showing guests to rooms) were carried out by the same staff who then served in the restaurant at peak mealtimes or performed housekeeping or room-cleaning tasks at other times of the day. The benefits of this to the firm were enormous: a reduction of core staff levels and the availability of a more resourceful workforce. Reduced staff levels also yielded significant cost benefits, since this is a labour-intensive industry. However, maintaining universal quality standards as the chain grew rapidly over a 25-year period became more and more problematic, especially when many new staff were recruited from other hotel groups with different working practices.

A system to monitor standard procedures was introduced in 1987. It regulated the thirteen main points of staff/customer interaction. These were: reservation, arrival/access, parking, check-in, hall, bedroom, bathroom/WC, evening meal, breakfast, shops, bar, outdoor games/swimming-pool and check-out. Each of these key interaction points was divided into a series of compulsory directives for staff, e.g. how to set out a bedroom, lay a place setting in the restaurant or welcome a guest. A booklet containing all 95 of these compulsory directives was issued to all staff and was a mainstay in the induction of new staff. An internal team of inspectors visited each hotel approximately twice each year to monitor standards. They functioned in the same way as 'mystery shoppers' in that they made reservations, arrived, stayed and departed incognito. On completion of their stay they would make themselves known to the General Manager (GM) for review and discussion. Percentage grades were awarded and recommendations made. This system, while helping Novotel to control and consolidate after a period of rapid growth, gradually became over-rigid and procedural in orientation.

At a meeting in 1992 for Novotel managers in an 'open space' format (i.e. where participants may propose topics for discussion, move from group to group according to preference, or indeed, leave) the relationship of hotel GMs and their staff teams was redefined from hierarchical to enabling. A new corporate slogan 'Back to the Future' ('Retour vers le futur') was adopted to reflect the outlawing of the bureaucratic style of standardisation and a return to Novotel's entrepreneurial roots. In addition, mixed level (i.e. beyond just the top team) working parties were established in three key issue areas: communication (marketing and image), management and commercial. Inter-functional groups were set up across hotels and countries. GM groups were established which clustered together special interests across countries, to share ideas, innovations or best practice. These GM interest groups were constructed around common hotel types within the Novotel chain, e.g. all GMs of motorway locations or airport locations or city centre locations.

The 95 directives were abolished as too rigid and replaced by three simplified general measures of performance – clients, management and people. All internal procedures were assessed only in relation to these three elements of the business. One and a half layers of management were eliminated, leaving only one direct reporting layer between GMs and the two co-presidents of Novotel. (Novotel now has just one chairman after the departure of Gilles Pelisson in the autumn of 1994, to help turn around Disneyland Paris.)

The role of the GM was rethought and redefined as capturing the spirit of 'maître de maison', much closer to the social role of a ship's captain. This led to a need for reassessment and redevelopment of all GMs, who were required to go through an assessment activity incorporating role-play in such situations as conflict resolution with subordinates or guests.

Whilst great effort was made to position these assessments and changes as constructive inputs for identifying positive training needs, rather than negative grounds for dismissal, this emphasis on new styles of working for both management and all staff created much anxiety and uncertainty which the top team had to transform into a positive atmosphere of empowerment and opportunity. As an illustration of the imaginative ways in which this extremely delicate problem was tackled, two Benedictine monks were guests at one of Novotel's large management conventions in 1993. The Benedictine fathers were invited to speak to the gathering about the principles of Benedictine hospitality and welcome which had graced their order since its founding 15 centuries before. Benedictine principles, duties and procedures were

Hotel chain Novotel drew on the centuries-old tradition of hospitality of the Benedictine order of monks when planning new working methods.

described and explained. It is also worth noting the continuous active involvement in the redevelopment process of the two original founders of Novotel (now co-presidents of the Accor Group), as well as the visible public involvement of the co-presidents of Novotel.

Activity 3.3

Consider the mini-case on the Novotel international hotel chain that you have just read. List the main items of organisational learning that occurred at Novotel.

(You may wish to refer to the article by Senge in the Course Reader.)

In your opinion, what are the key capabilities that Novotel now possesses as a result of the changes and developments described?

Discussion

In summarising the outcomes of the process change described above, both the structure and operations of Novotel's corporate headquarters, as well as operations and routines in every hotel in the chain, were transformed, although in differing degrees and over different timescales. The transformations reflect the new roles and tasks of management (managerial capabilities) shown in Table 3.3.

Table 3.3 New roles and tasks of management

Top management	Middle management	Front-line management
Creator of purpose and challenger of status quo	Horizontal information broker and capability integrator	Entrepreneur and performance driver

(Adapted from Bartlett and Ghoshal, 1993, p. 44)

Potentially sustainable sources of advantage for Novotel arising from the changes include the following:

- *Delayering has led to reduction in numbers of management and staff per hotel. Labour costs in the hotel business are significant; so also is time for staff to be available to deal with customers. The benefit is measurable in added value to staff and customers, and in the management of costs.*

- *Information flows throughout the company have changed. Flattening the hierarchy enables more relevant information to be conveyed faster.*
- *The role of headquarters has changed. It now acts as an information co-ordinator, collator and channel, rather than the instigator of time-consuming demands for central performance statistics. This releases GMs' time for driving performance. For example, the headquarters filters useful information to all hotels which they store for shared reference.*
- *Collaboration across and between levels has increased. GMs organise self-help clusters; training sessions are shared across the group; 'reflective clubs' ('clubs de réflexion') have been created in some hotels as mixed informal groupings of staff who meet to discuss innovations. Significantly, they contain staff from across all service areas and discussion covers the hotel as a whole, not the specific responsibility of any individual staff.*
- *The role of the GM has changed to that of 'coach', optimising the service and amenities available to guests by developing the competences of his or her team.*
- *Ways of working have changed for all staff. The horizons of staff have been broadened, giving greater awareness of the business as a whole as well as more responsibility, encouraging cross-functional links and increased autonomy, which adds value for staff and guests alike.*

3.5 CAPABILITIES AND CHANGE

Throughout Section 3, first in the discussion sections and then in the Novotel mini-case, we have been exploring what is meant by resources and capabilities and what organisations do with them in practice to implement their strategies and improve their performance.

In the Novotel case you have seen an example of how a company had to adjust itself not once, but over and over again, to changes in its business context. Each time it had to review what it was doing, why it was doing it that way and how effective it was relative to what its customers wanted. Novotel's top management had to continually review and monitor its positioning, its hotels, its internal procedures and processes. What at one point in the development of the business had been considered excellent, gradually became average or even substandard as the market developed and customer expectations continued to rise. Costs were rising too; competition was becoming more effective. It was not that the company was doing anything particularly bad, just that capabilities which had been developed under one set of conditions became inappropriate when those conditions changed. This illustrates the 'dynamics' of strategy.

A sense of dynamics is critical in strategy because strategies are always being developed and refined, reviewed and implemented against a set of moving targets which combine every aspect of industry conditions. Industries change, markets change, competitors change or may become partners in certain activities. How these changed industry dynamics and competitive dynamics affect current and future resources and capabilities has already been illustrated in Book 3.

Reflection: the sustainability of resources

In Book 3, you were asked to consider what the 'dynamics' of your own industry had been over the last decade. Had things stayed the same? How had any changes affected the sustainability of your organisation's market position and market share? At this point in our discussion of capabilities and change, think back to your answers to those earlier questions. Now consider the following additional questions:

- Which, if any, of your organisation's resources and capabilities have enabled you to retain or improve your position?
- Which, if any, of your resources or capabilities have been eroded or by-passed?
- Try to explain clearly why and how this has occurred.
- Also try to specify clearly what your organisation has done, or is doing, to refocus or rebuild its resource base.

We are surrounded by examples of this relationship between industry dynamics and competitive dynamics. Charities in the UK have had to rethink their fund-raising procedures, objectives and strategies in the light of competition for the public's charitable purse since the National Lottery was launched by the government. It has been some time since the charities could be adequately managed by inexperienced managers without proper financial or human resource skills and training, or since they could be effectively staffed by altruistic voluntary staff alone. Despite being not-for-profit organisations, they operate in a resource context which is highly competitive (especially for funds) and in which demand often outstrips supply. Similarly, the expectations held by the public of a police service frequently contain political, religious and social subtexts which have affected their relationship with racial or religious minority groups. The recruitment, selection and training of police officers has had to undergo fundamental redesign as a result of changes in the mix of the population, changes in government policy and priorities, and the emergence of entirely new categories of crime (such as computer hacking and sophisticated types of financial fraud) which have necessitated a rebalancing of resources and capabilities fit for such purposes.

Within both local government and national government, changes have been widespread, affecting the fit between changed environment and existing resources and capabilities. For example, within Europe, local government officers have had to develop capabilities which include understanding how the EU functions, in order to respond to the movement of many sources of funding from national government to European Commission departments.

Utilising resources to build capabilities is not a 'once-for-all' exercise. It is a continuous process. What gives this process a sense of direction are the dynamics of the context in which the organisation is trying to survive and succeed. In the next section we will look at some of the ways that organisations try to manage these continuous challenges to success and survival.

4 The boundaries of the organisation

Again and again in earlier sections of this book, issues have arisen concerning the ownership of resources. By this we do not just mean who owns particular resources, such as technical knowledge or a patent. More important, in strategic terms, is the question of whether an organisation needs to *own* the resource at all.

The point to emphasise is that organisations do not need to own all the resources they use – they simply need to ensure that they have access to them, together with the *internal* capability to manage them effectively. Therefore, whereas resources may be internal or external to an organisation, *capabilities are always internal.*

Think back once again to the airline take-off and landing slots, the scientific know-how of the research staff at SATRA, or the 'influence' network of the Lebanese chief executive. The organisation needs to ensure merely that the resources it needs are available and secure to be used when it needs them. It is therefore more a matter of 'control' than of ownership. Ownership may be necessary in order to ensure adequacy and frequency of access to a critical resource. Or it may be possible to pay another organisation which owns the resource to rent it to you for a fee instead.

In this section we will discuss the implications of the resource-based view of strategy for the size and scope of organisations. What should they do for themselves and what should they resource from outside? Where should the boundaries be drawn? Does it matter? You may recognise that we are returning to the 'make or buy' (in-source or out-source) issues that we first discussed in Section 3.1. There are also links to the discussion of 'classical', 'sport' and 'relational' contracts in Book 2.

It is useful to indicate the strategy concepts which are relevant here. They include: all corporate-level strategy, transaction cost analysis, time-path dependency and the value chain. These will be discussed in turn.

This section will also look at the consequences of the boundaries of the organisation for managing critical resources effectively, over the long term. That means a consideration of capability-building and the management of learning (i.e. to manage the capability to keep building capabilities).

4.1 Corporate strategy issues: organisations or 'virtual' organisations?

In Book 1 you were introduced to the three levels of strategy in an organisation. Strategy at the level of the corporation was discussed as the management of the organisation's activities as a corporation, to gain maximum benefit from the organisation as a collection of related or unrelated businesses. At the corporate level lie the strategic decisions affecting the total portfolio of businesses which make up the organisation. It is primarily about the scope of the corporation, its geographic market spread and its product market spread and degree of vertical integration. It therefore defines the industries and markets in which the corporation competes, and the shape of the organisation which will enable it to do so most effectively, by means of the following:

- the overall scope of the organisation
- how it is to be run (its financial and organisational structure)
- how to allocate resources across and between business units
- merger, acquisition, diversification, demerger, divestment decisions affecting the business mix.

This has been a very lively strategy arena for most public-sector and not-for-profit organisations in recent years. Redesign of local authority governing structures has led to some organisations expanding in scope, while others shrink, both in resources and in business mix. Departments and whole authorities have been merged or divested, sometimes as agencies and sometimes as management buy-outs. Similarly, some charities, schools or hospitals are engaged in merger activity to reallocate resources across a wider geographic or market segment. For example, some private schools have merged their boys' and girls' schools to benefit from scale and scope economies – to use their resources more fully and intensively.

4.1.1 Vertical integration or 'quasi-integration'?

These changes have often affected the set of vertical relationships in which the organisation is involved. Many of the set of vertically linked activities in which local government, schools, hospitals or military establishments are involved, are now managed by 'quasi-integration'. Quasi-integration means a long-term relationship that may take the form of a written contract. Alternatively it may take the form of an understanding between the parties as to their mutual expectations. The idea of 'quasi' as opposed to full integration is that you can achieve the same amount of influence or control and the same objectives from organisations without the legal ownership usually implied by vertical integration.

A well-known example of such quasi-integration is that between the UK retailer Marks and Spencer and its suppliers. These are particularly long-standing relationships, many lasting for decades. Although acknowledged as a very demanding customer by its suppliers, these long-term relationships are widely regarded as contributing greatly to the reputation of that company for high-quality products and service. Such a relationship as that between Marks and Spencer and its supplier network is an example of what we defined earlier as a 'virtual' organisation – separate organisations which are dependent upon each other for performing important parts of their activities, and so have many shared interests and resources. Benetton has a similar network of relationships.

The idea contained in the concept of a 'virtual' organisation is that firms are as frequently involved in *collaborative* networking behaviour as in *confrontational* competitive behaviour. Collaboration amongst organisations appears to be increasing rather than diminishing. That is in response to a range of external environmental and internal resource pressures, which are making it difficult for one organisation to contain within its own organisational boundaries all the resources necessary to meet its customers' needs in the long term. For example, there is no car company in the world today which is not involved with one or more of its direct competitors at some point in its value chain. It may be for research into fuel economy, or the design of a new gearbox. These joint ventures and other types of collaborative alliances are partly driven by cost and partly by scarcity of specialist resources. The factors causing such collaboration will be discussed more fully later in the course.

4.1.2 Transaction costs and the scope of the firm

You should now read pages 374–378 in the Set Book, the sections entitled, 'Economies of scope', 'Economies from internalizing transactions', and 'Information advantages of the diversified corporation'.

Vertical integration forces us to think about some of the most critical strategic issues facing any organisation. We have already discussed them at some length in Section 3.1 in our review of transaction costs. The concept of transaction costs helps us to decide where to draw the boundaries of the organisation and why. For example, Microsoft may be totally reliant on IBM's PC architecture and Intel's chips, but it certainly does not need to own them. By contrast, American Express may wish to keep its IT function in-house rather than to out-source, because it regards its database management capability as a strategic asset and wishes to retain internal control over it. In this case the IT function and systems are regarded not as routine, but as strategic and therefore important not just for current business needs but also for the future development of the business. Table 3.2 summarised the conditions under which either (external) markets or (internal) hierarchies are likely to be preferable in any organisation.

Reflection

In order to be clear about some of the consequences of factors affecting the scope of the firm, compare Novotel's ownership and strategic use of its worldwide reservation systems with SAS's lack of control over its system.

4.2 DYNAMIC CAPABILITIES ISSUES: BUILDING ORGANISATIONAL CAPABILITY

Book 3 discussed the sustainability of resources and capabilities over the longer term, against industry dynamics which affect their long-term viability.

You were asked about the 'dynamics' of your own industry over the last decade and to consider which, if any, of your organisational resources or capabilities had been eroded, and what your organisation is doing to rebuild its resource base. In this section we will look further at such issues as:

- the role of organisational learning and organisational routines in building and sustaining distinctive capabilities
- organisational knowledge flows for sharing knowledge within and between firms.

Miyazaki (1995, pp. 16–17) provides a delightful and simple illustration of the process of building capabilities which will be reproduced here almost in full. She describes the owner of a small café in England who specialises in cooking fried breakfasts including sausage and chips, fried egg and chips, omelette and chips and other similar menu items. His customers are requesting new dishes such as moussaka. The café owner cannot decide which new dish to offer and eventually decides he has no skill in any of them. A friend suggests that he makes a list of what he is good at, that is his capabilities. The list includes:

- purchasing good quality materials such as potatoes, eggs, bread and raw sausages
- producing good quality products at speed, specifically fried eggs, fried chips, grilled sausages and toast
- listening to customers' preferences.

On consideration of this list, he finally has an idea of what to do that will build on his existing capabilities and also develop additional capabilities over time. He will add hamburger with chips and cheese omelette with chips to his menu within two weeks. He has decided that grilling hamburgers is similar to grilling sausages. Also, selecting raw sausages is likely to help him in selecting good raw minced meat. He will have to learn how to season and cook the hamburger, but feels confident that his existing skills in cooking omelettes will enable him to cope with cheese omelettes easily. He also decides that in three months' time he will add moussaka to the menu as a totally new dish which he can practise in his spare time. Some of the skills required to make moussaka, such as frying aubergines, are completely new to him. However, some draw on existing skills, such as chopping onions.

This simple example of capability-building for an individual illustrates the point that capability-building is 'time-path-dependent' and also cumulative – it takes time and effort and needs to build on what has gone before.

Another way of understanding this, for an organisation rather than an individual, is to think of the organisation as a tree. The roots of the tree represent basic resources; the trunk of the tree represents time-path-dependent learning; and the branches represent various capabilities. New branches are always growing and sprouting new leaves, just as organisations should always be able to evolve new capabilities from new combinations of resources and trajectories of learning pathways.

4.2.1 Organisational learning and organisational routines

Learning and innovation is often dependent on what Kay (1993) calls the 'internal architecture' of an organisation, rather than being solely technology- or R&D-dependent. Kay uses the term 'architecture' to describe relationships, both formal and informal, amongst staff (internal networks), with customers and suppliers and inter-firm collaborative arrangements (external networks). Architecture is the conduit for organisational knowledge and routines. The existence of these relationships is not a revelation; in fact they are often taken for granted. This architecture should benefit organizations seeking to obtain economics of scope through the transfer of capabilities across and between different businesses. Indeed, the point is that their importance can easily be overlooked.

Some well-known examples of this type of capability transfer come from the US multinational Procter and Gamble (P&G). The first example is one of transferring a technical capability. As a result of research carried out in Europe in the 1980s for the European market, the formula for a new liquid detergent was so much improved that the technical know-how was transferred to their research centre in the USA and used to improve a similar product already launched in the American market, but not particularly successfully. As a result of the improved research from Europe, P&G's American technical research scientists were able to incorporate improved performance features into the product designed for the US market. The product was subsequently re-launched and became a category leader in its segment. It was the intra-organisational transfer of learning which made this possible.

A second example from P&G concerns its human resource management. As the European market for consumer goods began to change and converge throughout the 1970s and 1980s P&G began to feel it necessary to respond by developing and marketing more Europe-wide products. However, its organisational structure was set up to be autonomous in each European country and the different management teams would not co-operate or share any information. So P&G began to experiment with Europe-wide teams to manage individual products on a Europe-wide basis. To begin with this was a disaster. The 'Euro-teams' were completely ineffectual and were largely ignored in the company. Adjustments were made to the Euro-teams which clarified their remit, enhanced the seniority level and the continuity of membership, and balanced the geographic representativeness of the leaders of each team. It took more than 15 years to make these teams work effectively. However, the company felt that this was an experience curve that it was obliged to travel. It is a learning trajectory that is now being followed and emulated by many rivals.

Some general points on the relationship between organisational learning, organisational routines and capabilities may be noted as follows:

- Capability transfer depends upon organisational learning and organisational routines.
- Knowledge represented by organisational learning will live in the organisation as organisational routines.
- Organisational routines contain both formal and informal, codified and tacit knowledge.

Miyazaki (1995) defines routines as 'patterns of interactions which represent successful solutions to particular problems'.

You should now re-read the Set Book, pages 125–126, the section entitled 'Capability as resource integration: direction and routine'.

This section in the Set Book discusses mechanisms for integrating and co-ordinating teams of resources, particularly human resource skills and knowledge. Two integrating mechanisms are discussed: rules and directives, and organisational routines. The first type is based on codified knowledge. The second type is based on 'regular and predictable patterns of activity made up of a sequence of co-ordinated actions by individuals' (Grant, p. 125). This implies that organisational routines involve a high degree of tacit knowledge. The role of management is to enable the development of routines to achieve integration and co-ordination of capabilities, just as in the P&G examples.

Organisational learning, and knowledge flows within firms, together with other process issues in strategy will be discussed further in Book 7.

Activity 4.1

Describe any 'organisational routines' (explicit or implicit) within your organisation for:

- building
- exploiting
- transferring or sharing
- sustaining
- blocking organisational capabilities.

4.3 OWNERSHIP, CONTROL OR JUST LINKS IN A CHAIN?

This discussion of the boundaries of the firm ends by revisiting the value chain. It is one of the simplest ways to understand the issue of where to draw organisational boundaries. The boundaries of the firm are synonymous with the decisions it has taken in constructing its value chain. One of the ways of understanding the range of strategic options available to an organisation is to see where it has chosen to cut its activities along the value chain. How vertically integrated has it chosen to be and why? This is the balance it has chosen between internal capabilities and external complementary assets.

Hall (1994) defines a functional capability as resulting from 'the knowledge, skill and experience of employees and others in the value chain'. Each value chain configuration embodies a different set of such knowledge and experience.

Go back once more to Figure 3.2, the Novotel business chain. Ask yourself whether it is necessary for Novotel to own its own worldwide central reservation system, situated outside Paris. It could access another reservation system, possibly the Sabre system belonging to American Airlines. Perhaps, in the view of Novotel's management, ownership of their own system (in fact it is owned by the parent company Accor) confers upon them the ability to construct other linkages within the firm or across the other chains in the Accor group of businesses. It makes it possible to transfer learning or enhance customer service or develop more targeted marketing initiatives. For Novotel this may be a resource on which they have built distinctive capabilities. They have chosen to construct their value chain in this way rather than another way. Their specific value chain configuration forms the basis of their competitive strategy. It is likely to be different from the configuration of other international hotel chains.

Similarly, if we return now to Benetton and consider once more the manufacturing and retail value chains in Figures 1.2 and 1.3, Benetton's sources of distinctiveness are clear. The boundaries of the two organisations, Novotel and Benetton, represent particular management decisions about how to design their value chains to maximise their respective potential sources of advantage and appropriate the best returns from that particular pattern of activities.

5 Summary and conclusion

In this book we have emphasised a number of things about the resource-based approach to strategy:

- that resources form the basis of capabilities
- that strategy analysis must include the identification of the cluster of resources of each organisation
- the notion of 'ownership' by organisations of distinctive capabilities, i.e. those which are unique to that organisation
- capabilities (to meet your organisation's objectives) are likely to be internal and owned, whereas resources may be either internal or external (not owned)
- that distinctive capabilities generate potential returns for the firm if they are sustainable and the returns are appropriable
- that it is from these distinctive capabilities that the variance of performance between firms in the same industry sector arises
- that the depreciation of resources (and the returns earned from them) necessitates the replenishment and upgrading of resources
- that organisational routines provide the basis for the exchange of skills, expertise and learning
- that human resources are critical in the resource-based approach to strategy
- that it is managers and managerial action which hold the key to creating organisational distinctiveness through building, developing and renewing capabilities.

This book has emphasised the following:

- the ability to exploit clusters of resources to create and accumulate new strategic assets more quickly and cheaply than competitors
- the organisational dynamics of identifying, building and sustaining non-tradable, non-imitable capabilities
- the organisational dynamics and routines to enable the application of capabilities, e.g. to innovation or to learning.

5.1 Objectives revisited

The purpose of this book has been to explore with you the resource-based approach to strategic thinking and strategic decision-making. Having completed your work on this book, you should be able to state the difference between a resource and a capability. More important, however, is that you have also learned from this book the difference between the two matters, and why, therefore, they are such powerful concepts in strategic thinking. It is your task as managers to transform your organisation's resources into the capabilities that will be the source of its future strengths.

REFERENCES

Amit, R. and Schoemaker, P. (1993) 'Strategic assets and organisational rents', *Strategic Management Journal*, Vol. 14, pp. 33–46.

Baden-Fuller, C., Calori, R. and Hunt, B. (1995) 'Novotel Case Study'.

Barney, J.B. (1991) 'Firm resources and sustained competitive advantage', *Journal of Management*, Vol. 17, No. 1, pp. 99–120.

Bartlett, C.A. and Ghoshal, S. (1993) 'Beyond the M-form: toward a managerial theory of the firm', *Strategic Management Journal*, Vol. 14, Special Issue, Winter, pp. 23–46.

Chandler, A.D. (1962) *Strategy and Structure*, MIT Press, Cambridge, MA.

Daft, R. (1983) *Organisation Theory and Design*, West, New York.

Grant, R.M. (1991) 'The resource-based theory of competitive advantage: implications for strategy formulation', *California Management Review*, Spring, pp. 114–135.

Grant, R.M. (1995) *Contemporary Strategy Analysis: concepts, techniques, applications*, 3rd edn, Blackwell, Oxford (the Set Book).

Hall, R. (1994) 'A framework for identifying the intangible sources of sustainable competitive advantage' in Hamel, G. and Heene, A. (eds) *Competence-Based Competition*, J. Wiley & Sons, Chichester.

Hofer, C.W. and Schendel, D. (1978) *Strategy Formulation: analytical concepts*, West Publishing Co., St. Paul, MN.

Kay, J. (1993) *Foundations of Corporate Success*, Oxford University Press, Oxford.

Lippman, S.A. and Rumelt, R.P. (1982) 'Uncertain imitability: an analysis of inter-firm differences in efficiency under competition', *The Bell Journal of Economics*, Vol. 13, No. 2, pp. 418–438.

Miyazaki, K. (1995) *Building Competences in the Firm: lessons from Japanese and European optoelectronics*, St Martin's Press, New York.

Nelson, R. and Winter, S.G. (1982) *An Evolutionary Theory of Economic Change*, The Belknap Press, Cambridge, MA.

Nonaka, I. (1991) 'The knowledge-creating company', *Harvard Business Review*, November–December, pp. 96–104.

Peteraf, M. (1993) 'The cornerstones of competitive advantage: a resource-based view', *Strategic Management Journal*, Vol. 14, pp. 179–191.

Polyani, M. (1966) *The Tacit Dimension*, Doubleday, New York.

Porter, M.E. (1985) *Competitive Advantage*, The Free Press, New York.

Prahalad, C.K. and Hamel, G. (1990) 'The core competence of the corporation', *Harvard Business Review*, May–June, pp. 71–91.

Quinn, J.B. (1992) *Intelligent Enterprise*, The Free Press, New York.

Rumelt, R. (1984) 'Toward a strategic theory of the firm' in Lamb, R. (ed.) *Competitive Strategic Management*, Prentice-Hall, Englewood Cliffs, NJ.

Rumelt, R. (1991) 'How Much Does Industry Matter?' *Strategic Management Journal*, Vol. 12, No. 3, pp. 167–185.

Schumpeter, J.A. (1934) *The Theory of Economic Development*, Harvard University Press, Cambridge, MA.

Segal-Horn, S. (1995) 'Core competence and international strategy in service multinationals' in Armistead, C. and Teare, R. (eds) *Services Management: new directions and perspectives*, Cassell, London.

Stopford, J. and Baden-Fuller, C. (1990) 'Corporate rejuvenation', *Journal of Management Studies*, Vol. 27, No. 4, pp. 399–415.

Teare, R. and Armistead, C. (1995) *Services Management: New directions, new perspectives*, Cassell, London.

Teece, D. (1980) 'Economies of scope and the scope of the enterprise', *Journal of Economic Behaviour and Organisation*, Vol. 1, No. 3, pp. 223–247.

Teece, D. (1982) 'Towards an economic theory of the multiproduct firm', *Journal of Economic Behaviour and Organisation*, Vol. 3, pp. 39–63.

Teece, D., Pisano, G. and Shuen, A. (1990) 'Firm capabilities, resources and the concept of strategy', University of California Working Paper EAP-38.

Williamson, O.E. (1975) *Markets and Hierarchies*, The Free Press, New York.

ACKNOWLEDGEMENTS

Grateful acknowledgement is made to the following sources for permission to reproduce material in this book:

Figures

Figure 2.1: Peteraf, M. A. and Kellogg, J. L. (1993) 'The cornerstones of competitive advantage: A resource-based view', Figure 3, in Schendel, D. (1993), *Strategic Management*, **14**(3), March 1993, Copyright 1993 by John Wiley & Sons, Ltd. Reprinted by permission of John Wiley & Sons Ltd; *Figure 3.1:* Grant, R. M. (1995) *Contemporary Strategy Analysis*, 2nd edition, Figure 5.10, Basil Blackwell Ltd; *Figure 3.2:* Teare, R. and Armistead, C. (1995) *Services Management: new directions, new perspectives*, Figure 1, Cassell PLC.

Table

Table 3.3: Bartlett, C. A. and Ghoshal, S. (1993) 'Beyond the M-Form: toward a managerial theory of the firm', Figure 2, in Schendel, D., Cyert, R. M. and Williams, J. R. (1993) *Strategic Management*, **14**, Winter 1993, Copyright 1993 by John Wiley & Sons, Ltd. Reprinted by permission of John Wiley & Sons Ltd.

Photographs

Page 18: The Guide Dogs for the Blind Association; *Page 22:* M. and C. Saatchi; *Page 38:* Buckfast Abbey, Buckfastleigh.

BOOK 5

CHOOSING STRATEGIES

Prepared by the B820 Course Team

MBA Strategy

Contributors to this book:

Eric Cassells
Geoff Mallory
Bob Marshall
Richard Mole
Lez Rayman-Bacchus
Susan Segal-Horn

Contents

1 **Introduction** — 5
   1.1 Learning objectives of this book — 5

2 **Strategy formulation and sources of competitive advantage** — 6
   2.1 Competition, performance and strategic fit — 6
   2.2 An introduction to strategic choice — 7
   2.3 Competitive advantage and corporate success — 10

3 **Generic strategies for pursuing competitive advantage** — 13
   3.1 Introduction — 13
   3.2 Porter's generic strategies — 13
   3.3 Cost-based strategies — 15
   3.4 Differentiation-based strategies — 17
   3.5 Generic strategies in perspective — 20
   3.6 Probing and elaborating the generic strategies — 21

4 **Strategic options for products and markets, old and new** — 25
   4.1 Present products, present markets — 26
   4.2 Present products, new markets — 27
   4.3 New products, present markets — 28
   4.4 New products, new markets — 28
   4.5 Example: New and old in retail banking — 29
   4.6 Boundaries and the choices between old and new — 30

5 **Testing strategic options and strategic choices** — 32
   5.1 Introduction — 32
   5.2 The tests of suitability, feasibility and acceptability — 32
   5.3 The tests of consistency, consonance, advantage and feasibility — 33
   5.4 Testing for efficiency, effectiveness, economy and equity — 35
   5.5 Risk and uncertainty in strategic choice — 35
   5.6 Future modelling and scenario planning — 37
   5.7 Risk, reward and superior profitability — 38

6 **Summary and conclusion** — 41

References — 43

Acknowledgements — 44

1 Introduction

This book is about how organisations choose strategies. It pays no regard to whether an organisation's strategy is planned in a deliberate way, or whether it emerges from a stream of decisions and actions by managers. These, and the issues of culture, power, and ethics which impact on a manager's choices, will be considered in Books 7 and 9 of the course. The purpose of this book is to explain the wide choice of strategies available and to identify criteria to aid the strategist's choice. These two things will help you think about the choice of strategy in your organisation, and how your organisation might pursue a successful strategy.

The first topic we will discuss is that of the sources of competitive advantage, in Section 2. This is a central concern of strategy, and any choice of strategy should be based on a grounded understanding of an organisation's advantages and how these may be best exploited. The exploitation of advantage through generic strategies is considered in Section 3, to identify the basic choices which face an organisation.

The identification of advantage and choice of generic strategy is not enough, however, to ensure a strategy is successful. For that, greater knowledge is needed about products and markets, for example, and we consider the significance of many of the strategic choices that must be made at this level of detail to implement strategy successfully in Section 4.

Finally, in Section 5, we identify a range of tests and selection criteria that can be used to evaluate possible strategies and which should help an organisation choose one with the best chance of success.

In this book we concentrate on the development of a strategy for a business unit. Other considerations often apply to the development of *corporate* strategy, that is strategies for multiple business units. These broader considerations were introduced briefly in Book 1 and will be dealt with in depth in Books 10 and 11. We will, however, make some reference to them in our discussion of competitive strategy and advantage.

1.1 LEARNING OBJECTIVES OF THIS BOOK

After studying this book you should be able to:
- further your understanding of the concepts of competition and strategic advantage
- critically evaluate several conceptual approaches to strategy formulation and strategic choice
- identify criteria and tests against which strategic options can be evaluated
- appreciate the inherent risk and uncertainty when choosing strategies.

2 Strategy formulation and sources of competitive advantage

2.1 Competition, performance and strategic fit

Superior performance is often expressed in terms of profitability or market share, which are essentially comparative measures. Organisations can and do, however, use a variety of other performance criteria, financial and non-financial. They may measure success in terms of the value of their assets or returns on equity, sales, investment or capital employed. They may also 'benchmark' themselves against similar organisations on non-financial ratios such as output per employee, awareness/favourability ratings and so on.

In thinking about organisational performance and how competitive strategies achieve success, you should bear in mind the discussion from Book 2 about organisational objectives. Shareholders probably assume that management strive daily to build shareholder value, whereas management may have other goals to meet. A taxpayer may assume that hospital consultants strive only to make patients better, when they may also have personal research objectives. Such multiple objectives naturally impact on the choice of strategy.

Objectives and performance indicators may be financial and non-financial. Some of these can comprise a 'basket' of weighted individual measures. For example, university 'league tables' can comprise a basket of student accommodation availability, drop-out rates, completion rates, graduate employment rates and so on, aggregated to form a single index. Not-for-profit organisations may deploy resources to achieve high ratings on these indicators as a means of seeking sustainable competitive advantage in the competition for resources.

As discussed in Book 1, management may seek a strategic 'fit' between the opportunities available in the competitive environment and the organisation's internal resources and capabilities. This does not imply the pursuit of some kind of equilibrium or co-existence among competitors. Rather, 'fit' is about exploiting some perceived environmental opportunity, based on a clear understanding of the organisation's distinctiveness and competitive advantage. For this it must understand *how* its resources and capabilities give it a competitive advantage in relation to the capabilities of its competitors. An organisation's profit potential depends on whether its managers can use or develop its internal resources and capabilities to fit the emerging external opportunities.

2.2 AN INTRODUCTION TO STRATEGIC CHOICE

The question arises: 'If an organisation knows that its strategy will surely adapt with the passage of time, is there a sense in which it does not know where it is going?' Putting the question another way, is there any purpose in formulating strategy when strategies and plans will change? The answer is surely 'yes', if we allow that an 'intended' strategy will evolve during its implementation. Of course there are limits on what constitutes a feasible strategy. The degrees of strategic freedom open to an organisation can be summed up in the three test questions that you met in Books 1 and 2.

Where are we now?

The organisation can be viewed as a set of present 'states', perhaps measured by headcount, assets and liabilities, market positions and so on. In summary, 'Where are we now?' concerns the organisation's current resources and capabilities, irrespective of whether it is strong or weak. Importantly, the strategies by which the organisation arrived at its present state are implicit in this question.

Where do we want to go?

'Where do we want to go?' is about strategic intent. It subsumes organisational 'wishes' (such as to be number one in a market) as well as the resource-based considerations that you met in Book 4. As always, these considerations are moderated by the wishes of the more powerful stakeholders.

How do we get there?

This is the area of strategic choice and will be the subject of the rest of this book. Strategic choice involves, among other things, the management of the boundaries of all three questions.

In answering these three questions, it is instructive to note how, in the decades since the 1970s, a range of strategic approaches have come and gone almost like fashions. In the late 1970s to early 1980s, it was fashionable for large industrial concerns to diversify into related areas. For example, BOC Industrial Gases in the UK acquired a string of companies that *used* gas (a 'forward' vertical integration strategy) such as fish farms (that use oxygen) and pizza chains (pizzas are chilled under nitrogen). In this respect, BOC was interpreting 'Where do we want to go?' in a very wide sense. The mid–late 1980s saw a divestment of these acquisitions as the notion of 'sticking to the knitting' became fashionable. BOC divested itself of everything except its 'core businesses'.

2.2.1 Limits on the formulation of strategies

In public and private not-for-profit organisations, the answer to the question 'Where do we want to go?' may be given or assumed. For example, a country's tax collection agency has strict limits placed on its freedom. 'Where do we want to go?' is circumscribed. In the case of some organisations, therefore, freedom to make strategic changes may be limited by constitutional or legal arrangements.

In contrast, some charitable organisations may suffer from a lack of focus in their mission and be particularly susceptible to being side-tracked, as they do not have the straightforward measure of profit as a gauge of ultimate success. 'Where do we want to go?' may be interpreted broadly. For example, a newly-appointed Chief Executive to a child telephone helpline organisation could take up new causes such as the rights of the unborn child, or a natural parent-tracing service for foster children. The organisation will have to find or divert resources from its current mission to pursue these causes. It may also find itself competing with other voluntary organisations for the same philanthropic resources.

A useful pair of frameworks for understanding some of the limits on strategic choice is *mandate analysis* and *stakeholder analysis* (Smith, 1994).

Mandate analysis

Mandate analysis is used both by public and private not-for-profit organisations. The purpose of the analysis is to clarify and be consistent about the boundaries between:

1. what must be done
2. what could be done
3. what must not be done.

In not-for-profit organisations, the minimum that must be done is usually documented in legislation, health regulations, trust deeds and so on. Clarification of what is not ruled out is particularly important, however. For example, the UK Driving Test Agency is mandated to provide driving tests, but there is no explicit restriction about, say, holding tests on a Saturday (a convenience for a working public) and charging a higher price. Alerting organisational members to what they *might* do can lead to valuable discussions about the constraints on strategy formulation. A boundary also needs to be set between what could be done and what must not be done. Smith suggests that efforts should be made to identify activities that might be regarded as natural extensions of current ones.

Stakeholder analysis

You will remember the discussion of stakeholder analysis in Book 2. One of the main reasons for performing a stakeholder analysis is that any formulated strategy would, of necessity, have to take account of the main power-wielding stakeholders. The way in which the main stakeholders measure the performance of the organisation now and in the future needs to be understood by the management, if they are to formulate strategies that will, as far as possible, be accepted by the stakeholders.

Activity 2.1

Carry out a mandate analysis for an organisation you are familiar with. Now compare this to the outcomes of the stakeholder analyses you carried out in Book 2. What are the main differences you see between stakeholder and mandate analysis?

Discussion

As suggested above, a mandate analysis will often turn to what is documented to identify what could, must and must not be done. The focus is on the legal and formal constraints, rights and duties that an organisation has. These documents, laws and regulations may be external or internal in nature.

For example, a UK public limited company quoted on the London Stock Exchange is defined as a legal 'person', bound by all UK Parliamentary and statutory law – not just company law. Thus, ferry-operating companies can be, and have been, charged with criminal manslaughter when their ferries sink due to recklessness or negligence. These companies are also subject to the devolved legal powers of regulatory agencies such as utility regulators, the Stock Exchange, financial services regulators and environmental protection agencies. They are subject to European legislation and regulation, other international law to which the UK government has subscribed, and to the laws of other countries in which they operate.

As a legal 'person', a UK company is also subject to the vast body of Common Law (such as the law of contract) and Equity (such as the law of trust) which is recorded in the findings of the judiciary over many centuries. Thus, the law of contract, if enforceable, will bind companies to perform contracts they have agreed to, with few exceptions. In the construction industry, for example, unfavourable major contracts can end up bankrupting companies. The law of trust is more open, but nevertheless creates a duty of (implied) trust on, for example, directors towards shareholders, creditors, employees, government and the company itself. Thus, directors can be personally liable to creditors if they continue to trade, concealing the company's position, after they know it is technically insolvent – essentially fraudulent trading.

Under company law, UK companies are required to write up their own constitution (their 'memorandum and articles of association') which further defines the company's mandate. Finally, the law provides that it is the directors' duty to create a system to manage the company effectively. Therefore, all the decisions made by the board of directors, policy set under this framework, regulation and procedure for implementation, become part of the mandate of the company, which should govern its behaviour and that of its employees.

Overall, mandate analysis offers a framework to analyse what an organisation should do. It implicitly considers the power and influence of various stakeholders as they are enshrined in formal and legal relationships.

When we review stakeholder analysis and some of the associated concepts in Book 2, however, we find an emphasis on the resources provided by stakeholders, the rewards they expect in return and the effective balance of power and influence between them. In Book 2 we identified many other sources of power that stakeholders bring to an organisation other than simply formal (or legal) sources of authority. There is, therefore, an important emphasis on unwritten rules and implied norms of behaviour in an organisation. Finally, the contract theory that we studied in Book 2 may help us to recognise situations where the documented mandate of a company is important ('classical' long-term contracting) and where expectations from repeated interaction and co-operation ('relational' long-term contracting) is more relevant.

2.3 COMPETITIVE ADVANTAGE AND CORPORATE SUCCESS

Kay (1993) asserts that *corporate success* derives from a *competitive advantage* – which may vary from one market or industry to another. Competitive advantage is based on *distinctive capabilities and strategic assets*. These assets and capabilities are most often derived from and matched with the *relationships* that the organisation has with its customers, suppliers, employees, the government and so on. This approach is summarised in Figure 2.1, below.

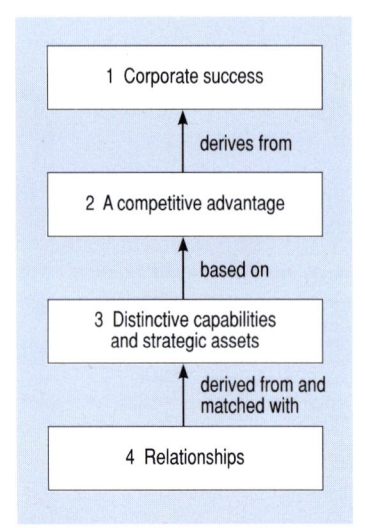

Figure 2.1   Sources of corporate success (adapted from Kay, 1993)

Why is competitive advantage necessary for success? To some extent, this depends on how we think about and measure 'success'. In economic terms, a useful measure of success is superior added value or 'rent' (Kay, 1993). 'Rent' can, by definition, only be achieved when the organisation is performing better compared with others in the same industry. If an organisation's capabilities and strategic assets are not distinctive, there is unlikely to be sustained advantage. On the other hand, distinctiveness is just a necessary, but certainly not sufficient, condition for competitive advantage, as we will see later.

Kay suggests that there are three types of distinctive capabilities:

- architecture
- reputation
- innovation.

Architecture is the term used to describe relationships, both formal and informal, between internal staff, with customers and suppliers, and inter-firm collaborative arrangements (networks). Architecture provides an effective conduit for organisational knowledge and routines, which are often the key source of sustainable competitive advantage (as we discussed in Book 4).

Reputation is built on relationships with an organisation's suppliers and customers. A particular reputation, perhaps for reliability or speed of service, is a source of advantage where a buyer values this reputation over a competitor's at the moment when a contract is placed. Reputations are, however, a wasting source of advantage if they are not maintained.

Innovation is Kay's third type of distinctive capability. Innovation can be a source of competitive advantage when it provides means for an organisation to compete more efficiently, offering a product which is more valuable to a customer; or when it allows the organisation to compete in new ways (for example, using new distribution channels). Innovation is only sustainable as an advantage, however, when it cannot be easily imitated or superseded by alternative innovations. Think back to the case of Biogen in the article by Eccles and Nohria in the Course Reader, for example, where pharmaceutical innovations were superseded by drugs with small chemical alterations; or Apple computer's GUI discussed in the mini-case in Book 4.

Competitive advantage can also derive from the organisation's ownership of strategic assets. *Strategic assets* can be classified as:

- *natural monopolies* such as scale economies, or closed systems compatibility standards such as the PC operating system from Microsoft, or proximity to high-value or low-cost inputs (rare minerals, a labour pool with particular skills, research laboratories or low-labour cost regions)
- *sunk costs*, such as prior investment in capital equipment (such as plant for oil and gas refining), knowledge, or established skills (for example, in managing large and complex projects)
- *exclusivity*, such as exclusive importation or distribution agreements, licences to use a particular technology, or legislative protection.

MINI-CASE: GLAXO AND ZANTAC

You will remember the introductory mini-case on Zantac in Book 1. If not, refresh your memory by re-reading it now. Glaxo was one of the cases studied by Kay as the basis for his ideas on the sources of advantage. Using Kay's terminology the following sources of advantage can be identified in the strategies adopted by Glaxo.

Innovation

Although Zantac was not a highly innovative product, Glaxo managed to convince doctors that it was innovative and worth paying a premium for. Perhaps more importantly, Glaxo pioneered a number of innovations in the way that the product was developed (reducing the development time through parallel engineering), produced (building a factory before regulatory approval was won) and launched (achieving near-simultaneous product launches internationally).

Architecture

Some of the innovations in product development, production and launching depended on a reconfiguration of the relationships between departments charged with R&D, obtaining regulatory approval and planning the marketing of Zantac. In addition, Glaxo were able to achieve rapid market penetration internationally by arranging a network of marketing and sales joint ventures and agencies to complement their own sales forces.

Strategic asset-exclusivity

Having achieved such a strong market position for Zantac, Glaxo are, of course, protected by patent and licence legislation from any other company exploiting the same chemical compound as a pharmaceutical drug for a period of twenty years.

> If these are the main sources of advantage that Glaxo exploited in developing Zantac, what of their future when the strategic asset of exclusive exploitation expires? Glaxo will be faced with a host of licensed 'generic' competitors who will undercut their prices. Will Glaxo have new or further sources of advantage it can exploit?
>
> - First, Glaxo has re-invested a higher percentage of its revenues (largely from Zantac) in researching a portfolio of new drugs. It must hope that the scale of its effort produces a new 'blockbuster' drug to replace Zantac although clearly this cannot be guaranteed.
> - Secondly, Glaxo has continued to excel in the rapid worldwide approval and launch of the new drugs it has developed. The unique arrangements and routines it has built up have continued to deliver advantage to it. This is clearly a distinctive capability.
> - Finally, Glaxo has gained a *reputation* as a very reliable, safe, effective and innovative brand with those doctors using Zantac. Glaxo must hope that this loyalty will transfer to new ethical drugs it launches.
>
> Glaxo's future after Zantac's patents expire remains uncertain, but Glaxo must hope it can continue to derive advantage from its *innovation*, *architecture* and *reputation*.

As the example of Glaxo and Zantac shows, the more successful companies often combine architecture, reputation, innovation and strategic assets to deliver competitive advantage. Much of Sony's success, for example, is attributed to the rotation of staff between different functions, its involvement of suppliers in manufacturing process design, its technical creativity in product innovations (such as merging electronic and mechanical technologies) and its established skills in miniaturising electronic products.

Note that competitive advantage involves organisations in finding some way of disturbing the bases of 'perfect' competition in an industry or sector. All organisations must compete in some way or other for scarce resources (indeed, the working capital provided by customers in commercial organisations is no more than a scarce financial resource with which to pay suppliers, wages and salaries, dividends, etc.). Monopoly providers such as UK universities are now forced to compete for students and research grants as universities in the USA have always done, and many charitable organisations are being driven to adopt strategies based on competition as the struggle for scarce funds intensifies.

Activity 2.2

At this point, you should read and make notes on Chapter 7 in the Set Book. While reading, list the key assumptions that Grant makes on the nature of competition. What does he have to say about competing in service-based industries? Pay particular attention to the section on sources of competitive advantage which we will discuss in the next section.

3 Generic strategies for pursuing competitive advantage

3.1 INTRODUCTION

As discussed in Book 3, organisations can achieve above-average profits, relative to *all* organisations, by locating in an attractive industry. Some industries with above-average profits, such as the drug abuse industry, tend, however, to operate outside socially acceptable and formally recognised legal frameworks! Others, despite attractive features, may be very difficult to enter. More commonly, the opportunity to earn supernormal profits within an industry depends on exploiting some competitive advantage *within that industry*. By casual observation, sources of competitive advantage seem infinitely variable. Competitors continually jostle for customer attention by adding more features or extra service at no charge, by cutting prices or supplying extra product at the same price. We regularly see airline advertisements claiming to service more destinations with more comfortable seating than competitors; business information providers claim more up-to-date statistics and business trends than other providers; courier services claim faster parcel delivery to more destinations than their competitors.

We have argued in this course that seeking competitive advantage is a key component of strategy. In the Set Book, Grant refers to the work of Michael Porter (1985) and his generic strategies of cost leadership, differentiation and focus. These are a useful way of identifying some generic approaches to exploiting competitive advantage, and are reviewed below.

3.2 PORTER'S GENERIC STRATEGIES

Porter's summary is shown in Figure 3.1 (overleaf).

We can summarise the features and scope of Porter's generic strategies in the following manner.

Cost leadership

Here the organisation sets out to be *the* low-cost producer in its industry, using any or all of the various sources of cost advantage. If an organisation can achieve and sustain cost leadership, then it will be an above-average performer in its industry, provided it can command prices at the industry average or increase overall sales volumes from lower prices. The organisation may price its offerings at a level that is comparable with, or lower than, its competitors but yet achieve higher gross margins. Note that superior profits and advantage derive from lower *cost*, not price. Low costs do, however, give an organisation increased flexibility on the pricing strategies it can pursue. Further, being the lowest-cost producer does not mean that the value package offered to customers is unimportant. The low-cost producer must offer a level of functionality and quality that is acceptable to its market sector.

	Competitive advantage	
	Lower cost	Differentiation
Broad target	• Cost leadership	• Broad differentiation
Narrow target	• Cost focus	• Differentiation focus

(Competitive scope on vertical axis)

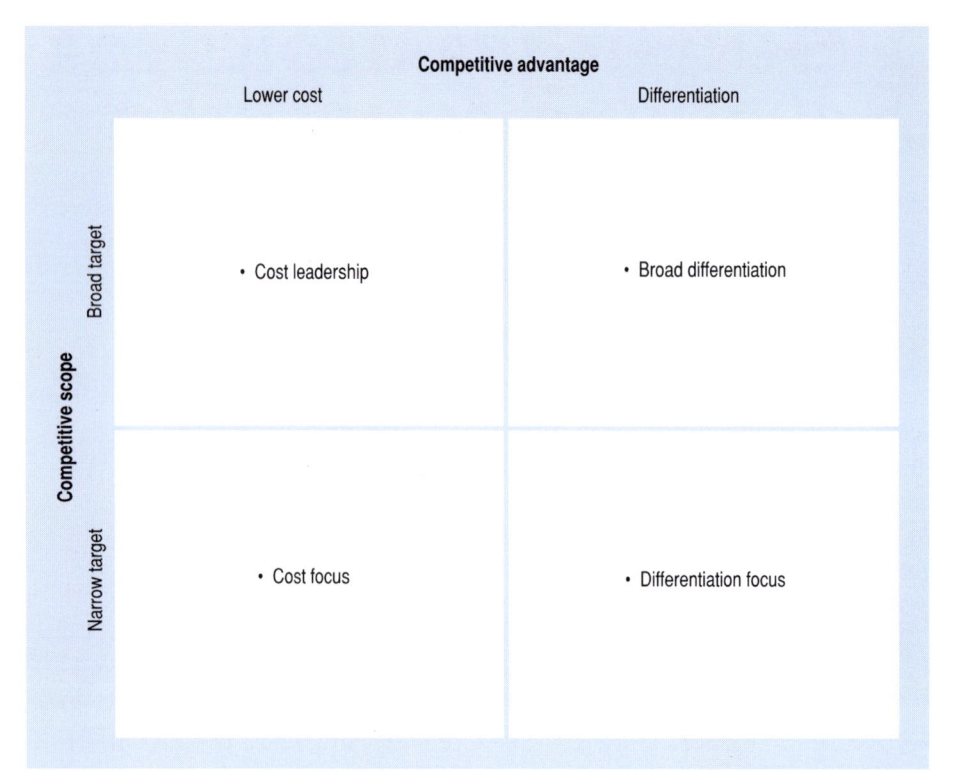

Figure 3.1   Porter's generic strategies

Differentiation

Here an organisation seeks to be unique in its industry along some dimensions that are valued by buyers. It selects one or more attributes that buyers in an industry perceive as important and uniquely positions itself to meet those needs. The means for differentiation are peculiar to each industry and each organisation. It is rewarded for its uniqueness with a premium price. A firm that can achieve and sustain differentiation will be an above-average performer in its industry provided its price premium exceeds the extra costs incurred in being unique. The product or service must continue to be valued by the customer if the price premium is to hold up. Of course, the differentiator cannot ignore cost, since a poor cost position will erode any gains that result from a price premium.

Focus

A firm may pursue advantage from cost leadership or differentiation, either in the broad market, or by pursuing a strategy of *focus*. Segments, or a group of segments, in an industry are selected for either a cost or a differentiation strategy, to the exclusion of other segments. By optimising strategy for the target segments, the focuser seeks to achieve a competitive advantage in its target segments. It aims to use its cost or differentiation strategy to out-focus its broadly-targeted competitors. This requires a clear appreciation of (a) where its focus is and (b) how narrow or broad a market segment or sector to compete in. A segment may be broadly defined by geographic coverage, product application, distribution channel, or particular customer characteristic (such as age, gender, ethnicity or income group).

Taking differentiation, cost advantage and focus together gives the four generic strategies shown in Figure 3.1: cost leadership, cost focus, broad differentiation and differentiation focus.

1 A cost leadership strategy involves being the lowest-cost producer across the broad sector or industry.
2 A cost focus strategy aims for cost advantage within a specific segment.
3 A broad differentiation strategy involves offering a differentiated product or service across a broad sector or industry.
4 A differentiation focus strategy aims for differentiation within a specific segment.

We now look in more depth at these generic strategies.

3.3 COST-BASED STRATEGIES

In the set book, Grant suggests that there are eight drivers of cost advantage:

- economies of scale
- economies of learning
- process technology
- product design
- process design
- capacity utilisation
- input costs
- residual differences in operating efficiency.

A broadly targeted *cost leadership strategy* is appropriate where significant economies of scale or scope are possible and where it is difficult to differentiate the product. Take oil refining and petrol distribution, for example. Here the industry structure has led to established practices for managing large capital investments and distribution channels are often shared. The competitive arena cuts across many markets and so the competitive scope is broad. This is also true for many cosmetics, such as soaps, deodorants, shampoos and after-shave lotions. These are promoted for everyday use by all sections of the population, at very competitive prices. Most of these products are likely to be mature in terms of their product life-cycles.

On the other hand a *cost focused strategy* is appropriate where a product or service is clearly defined and offered in a budget-conscious market segment. This strategy depends on the existence of segments whose needs are for products or services with fewer functional features than those aimed at the broad market. The YMCA and YWCA provide examples of 'cost focus' strategies that aim to provide minimum-cost accommodation to young people. Although they attract travellers with different motivations – the temporarily homeless, tourists, low-pay trades people – their common denominator is an overriding concern for the basics of decent accommodation at minimum cost. Then again, car manufacturers such as Lada and Hyundai have established themselves in Western markets by targeting a segment of the population whose needs for personal transport are relatively modest, with extremely low prices. The manufacturers of these cars rely on older-generation technologies and low input costs, such as low labour rates and unsophisticated manufacturing processes.

The Lada Samara hatchback – a strategy of using older technology to produce low-price cars for a specific segment of the market

Cost control is clearly central to competitive strategy, whether the organisation is pursuing a strategy of cost advantage or differentiation. A sensible programme for cost reduction is not the same as pursuing a strategy for cost advantage, however. Competitors may also be seeking a cost advantage, and there may be a jointly shared interest in making an assessment of their own cost position in relation to others.

While most managers would agree that the control of cost is critical to their organisation's health, there is often wide disagreement within the organisation about what those costs are. Furthermore, the cost behaviour of a product or service tends to be poorly understood in terms of knowing how the real costs affect profitability. In some instances, a firm's allocation of costs to its various activities may remain unchanged for a decade or more despite obvious changes in the activities themselves. In addition, firms often have very little understanding of their competitors' cost position, which is essential for understanding their own *relative* cost position. What is needed is a systematic analysis of cost to determine an organisation's cost position *relative* to its competitors and to identify ways that an organisation may gain sustainable cost advantage. Existing accounting systems have a limited role here.

Activity 3.1

Think of several examples of organisations pursuing cost-based strategies.

Now read and make notes on Chapter 8 in the Set Book. Do the organisations that you have identified in the previous part of this activity derive their cost advantages from the sources identified in this chapter?

How could you analyse the costs of a competitor in your industry? In the public or not-for-profit sector, how could you establish the costs of an organisation which delivers a similar service?

3.4 DIFFERENTIATION-BASED STRATEGIES

When following a strategy of *broad differentiation* it is important to strike the right balance between providing unique benefits while minimising the additional cost of the product or service. Getting the balance wrong could result in the erosion of all superior profits. Honda seeks competitive advantage by following a differentiated strategy in terms of enhanced reliability and advanced engine and transmission technologies. Its competitive scope is broad, because it competes globally and across all market segments. Another example of a 'differentiation' strategy is the Swatch Watch that is available through retail channels such as jewellers, department stores and airport shops. To its broad market it is differentiated by its modern and unusual designs. As the designs have changed, a thriving collectors' market has developed.

The Porsche 911 Carrera Cabriolet – product of a strategy of differentiation

An organisation may choose a strategy of *differentiation focus* when a target segment has unique needs and is willing to pay a premium for the right product or service features. This strategy depends on the existence of segments whose needs are for products or services with greater functional or service features than those aimed at the broad market. Here, customers expect or are offered a comprehensive product package, including service features if needed. The competitor operating in this segment is likely to seek out sophisticated design and technologies, whether related to a product or a service. The manufacturers of high-performance cars such as Porsche, Maserati or Lamborghini, for example, are highly differentiated in their aesthetic design, their advanced handling and other sought-after features. They serve a small clientele of enthusiasts drawn from all over the world.

Since differential advantage depends on whether potential customers value their relationship with the supplying organisation, the scope for being differentiated is not restricted to extra features on the product or service. There may be scope for differentiating the organisation's relationship with its customers in many ways:

- delivering the product or service
- managing the customer's inventory
- financing to help purchase
- training new users

- removing barriers to the ordering process, trial periods, etc.
- establishing close partnerships with customers that facilitate just-in-time scheduling, open book accounting, joint efficiency seeking projects, organisational process development projects, and so on
- providing after-sales service.

These tangible aspects are accompanied by intangible qualities that potential customers weigh up in their evaluation of the relationship. For example, we noted previously that consumers exercise choice on the basis of the image they associate with a particular product, as is common in fashion goods. Or, to take a different example from financial services, there are investors who trade only in shares of companies that are deemed not to harm the environment.

A supplier, whether firm, charity or public service, and its customers are each party to an explicit or tacit contract of expected performance. Suppliers promise, and customers expect, that a product or a service will meet certain levels of quality, reliability, durability, safety and so on. The contract may be underpinned by regulatory constraints such as safety standards that today affect most products and services. Many complex products and services need to comply with both regulatory and voluntary criteria, otherwise there is a risk of chaos and reduced safety. Examples include standardised power socket dimensions, computer data protocols, car fuel lead levels and so on. However, while these performance criteria constrain differentiation in particular directions, such constraints are also very often sources of innovation. For example, without common standards, competitors' resources are often diverted to maintaining proprietary standards, and customers generally do not value proprietary standards. On the other hand, where there are common technical standards, competitors can focus their creativity on other areas that potential customers *are* likely to value.

In the same way, market segments are not just static structural characteristics of a market to be taken for granted. The reality is that market segments exist because of patterns to human behaviour, which organise and guide suppliers' thinking about how to differentiate themselves. People buy fashion accessories and cosmetics because they seek a particular identity. Segmentation is thus created and routinely maintained jointly by suppliers and buyers. While such segmentation can be stable over time, competitive forces lend segments a degree of fragility. This is a potential source of innovation, and fragility provides scope for further differentiation if the organisation is able to enlist potential customers in creating a new segment.

Activity 3.2

Think of several examples of organisations pursuing differentiation strategies. **Now read and make notes on Chapter 9 in the Set Book**. Do the organisations that you have identified in the previous part of this activity derive their differentiation advantage from the sources identified in the chapter?

How could you analyse the ways in which a competitor in your industry differentiates its product or segments its market? What might constitute differentiation advantage in the public or not-for-profit sectors? How would you identify such sources of differentiation advantage in not-for-profit organisations?

MINI-CASE: GENERIC STRATEGIES IN THE CAR INDUSTRY

Consider the competitive strategies adopted by car manufacturers serving the Western European market-place.

In the market for larger family and company cars, it is obvious that there is little differentiation between models such as the Nissan Primera, Peugeot 406, Toyota Avensis, Opel Vectra and Ford Mondeo. All have similar functionality and pricing is broadly the same. The manufacturers are primarily interested in selling significant volumes of these cars to benefit from scale-driven cost and learning advantages. These can seem to be best positioned as pursuing cost-based strategies (although only one, of course, can be a 'leader' – if we are to take the framework literally).

Staying in the larger family and company car market, there are other manufacturers charging a premium for cars which might be best described as brand differentiators, selling across the market but selling additional distinctive features. Rover, for example, has been driven by its lower volume to stress its traditional image, exemplified by its nostalgic grille on the premium-priced Rover 600. The same underlying design of car is sold by Honda as the Accord, with a premium being charged for the brand image of engineering excellence and reliability built up by the company. In the same way, cars such as the BMW appeal to those in the broad market who value the record of 'build' excellence BMW have built up.

We have already discussed cars such as the Lada and Hyundai which generally appeal to lower income segments who are willing to sacrifice functionality. These cars tend to rely on older technology: in Malaysia, Proton cars have similarly relied on technology acquired from Mitsubishi. Perhaps a more interesting example is the Fiat Cinquecento, a new technology small car designed as a city car with restricted functionality and using the locational advantage of being built using low-cost labour in Poland. In the same way, Mercedes and Swatch have a joint venture to build a city car for the next century.

In the differentiation focus section of the matrix, there is a group of cars which add luxury and prestige to the value-package purchased by consumers of very large family and company executive cars. These are cars such as Mercedes (any saloon), Jaguar, the BMW 525, the Alfa Romeo 166 and Saab 9–5. Another group of cars that are sold to distinct segments who are willing to pay a premium are the sports cars, such as the Mazda MX-5, BMW Z-3,

The Rover 618 (left) and Honda Accord (right) – two cars with the same underlying design aimed at different market segments

> MGF, Fiat Barchetta and Alfa Romeo Spider and GTV. This last group of cars differs in that the segment is interested in particular features (sporting abilities and image) and is willing to sacrifice some functionality (passenger space, luggage carrying, protection from the weather) to obtain it.
>
> If we now allocate these examples of generic strategies to Porter's framework, we can plot them as in Figure 3.2.

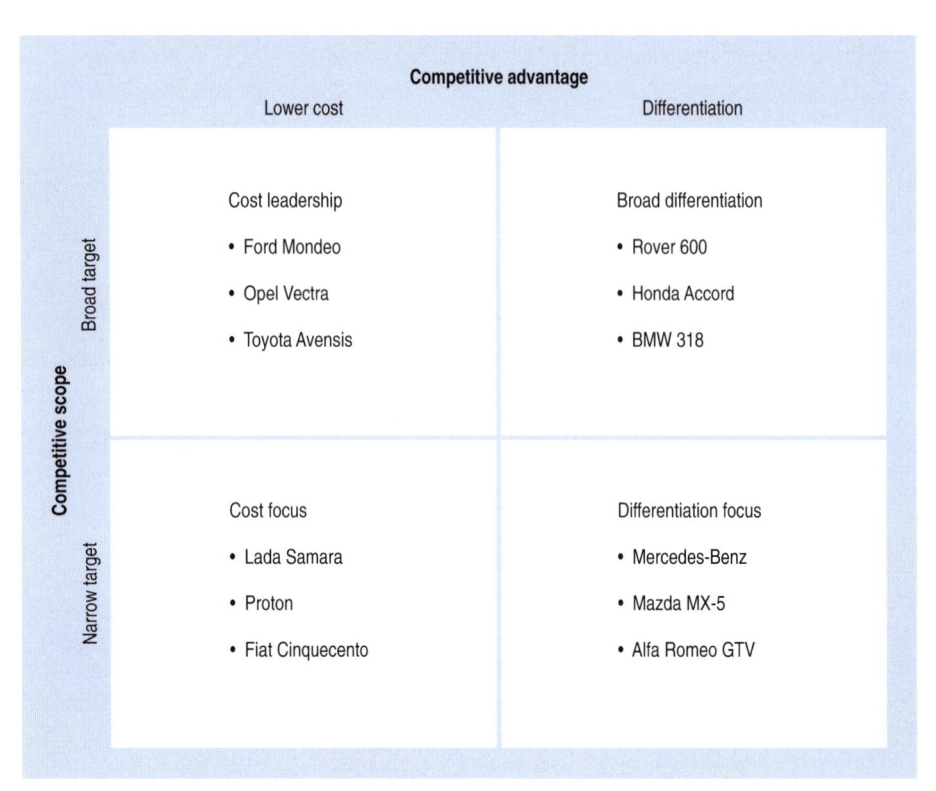

	Competitive advantage	
Competitive scope	**Lower cost**	**Differentiation**
Broad target	Cost leadership • Ford Mondeo • Opel Vectra • Toyota Avensis	Broad differentiation • Rover 600 • Honda Accord • BMW 318
Narrow target	Cost focus • Lada Samara • Proton • Fiat Cinquecento	Differentiation focus • Mercedes-Benz • Mazda MX-5 • Alfa Romeo GTV

Figure 3.2 Examples of generic strategies in the Western European car market

3.5 GENERIC STRATEGIES IN PERSPECTIVE

In Porter's view, the choice of generic strategy depends on the forces within the industry structure. The competitive environment tends to weed out inappropriate competitive strategies and their organisations on the basis of survival of the fittest. You have already encountered alternative views in Book 4 about the sources of competitive advantage, and further ideas will be presented to you in Book 6. The Porter framework does, however, help in the assessment of the relative strengths and weaknesses of competitors and therefore suggests what strategy a new entrant might follow to position itself, or how an established firm could reposition itself. In assessing the possibilities, a firm would need to consider a range of issues including:

- Are there 'differentiators' that are serving a segment at unnecessarily high costs?
- If there is no lowest cost producer in the sector and no apparent differentiation among competitors, does this mean that there is room for a 'differentiator' or 'cost leader'?

- Is there a fundamentally different way of competing that would reward a new entrant?

Stable industry environments, for example, may encourage cost advantage from scale and experience economies, as they move toward standardisation practices. Unstable environments may encourage differentiation more than cost advantage. For example, rapid and continual technological change in the information technology and telecommunications sectors is characterised by an ever-growing range of products and services. In this environment, new firms enter and leave the industry at a high rate, due to intense competitive rivalry and rapid technological change that often makes products obsolete before they can recover their investment.

In public sector and not-for-profit organisations, such as local government or public health care, broad cost-driven strategies are usually practised on the grounds of equity. It is not usually possible to obtain a differentiated service by payment of a premium, although there might well be a willing market. This may be seen as queue-jumping in an environment where services are rationed. During the current move towards privatisation and market-based reform in these sectors, private providers focus almost exclusively on providing differentiated service such as higher standards of hospital food, more frequent or convenient uplift of waste by local authorities and so on. It could be argued that raising consumer sensitivity to differentiable services will lead to increased sensitivity to value for money, and also, by contrast, to the idea of paying extra for extra services.

Activity 3.3

What generic strategies is your organisation pursuing? Different units in your organisation may be pursuing different strategies but, using Porter's ideas, identify these strategies and list the reasons for your categorisation.

3.6 PROBING AND ELABORATING THE GENERIC STRATEGIES

Porter's generic strategies are clearly useful for understanding competitive advantage and they have been very influential. Nevertheless, it is important to critically evaluate their strengths and weaknesses.

Bowman and Asch (1996) find significant problems in practice with the static nature of Porter's analysis in a complex and dynamic world. For example, cost leadership is often confused with competing in low-price segments and so the question of *where* to compete can be misleading if combined with the question of *how* to compete. It is irrelevant to compare Hyundai with Jaguar because they compete for different customers. Hyundai competes with firms who are perceived by the customer to offer competing products, such as Lada.

Bowman and Asch also suggest that inputs can get confused with outputs. Customers do not particularly care about the input side of a strategy, which is invisible to them. A cost leadership strategy, or even a low-cost producer strategy, is unlikely to be identified as such by the consumer. Cost leaders can gain superior profits from an average market price for an average product, based on their lower costs. Following this practice, cost leaders would probably enjoy an average market share and not gain the volumes necessary to secure 'experience curve' benefits, another route to securing costs.

In the same way, it appears that not all 'differentiators' command or demand premium prices. Some 'differentiators' actually increase market share instead. Differentiation in the airline industry – for example, by British Airways or American Airlines – has usually been aimed at increasing the number of passengers carried at similar prices to competitors. This is because the high fixed cost and capacity availability structure of running aircraft flights encourages airlines to maximise overall revenues, rather than a notional profit margin per passenger.

There are other dangers in using the generic strategies framework in too literal or rigid a manner. First, it is a static classification device. It takes no account of the way advantage is created and destroyed over time, in the way we discussed in Book 3 (and will elaborate on in Book 6). Secondly, there is a danger in trying to force organisations exclusively into one box or another. There needs to be a finer grain of analysis in practice to identify what an organisation's underlying sources of advantage actually are. This is why the Set Book chapters detail the sources of advantage that can underpin cost- and differentiation-based generic strategies. Organisations may even gain overall advantage by pursuing *both cost and differentiation advantages*, while being the leader in neither.

For example, the greatest profits in the UK supermarket sector during the period 1985–1995 were consistently achieved by Sainsbury. During this period, Sainsbury charged premiums over most competitors for own-label produce. They were not, however, the largest premiums in the sector. Sainsbury also pursued a low-cost strategy based on operational and managerial efficiencies, experience and scale benefits. They were not, however, the lowest-cost producer. Sainsbury was neither the leading differentiator nor the cost leader. By a careful blend of both strategies, however, the retailer achieved a period of prolonged competitive advantage resulting in superior profits.

Miller (1986) suggests that, in order to achieve differentiation, cost advantage and focus, we must consider how the organisation's fixed and current assets are being used. For example, in order to achieve a cost advantage, the organisation's assets tend to be selected and organised to maximise efficiency – Miller calls this *asset intensity*. But for a differentiator to achieve superior returns, there is an observed tendency to squeeze the maximum variety out of the minimum of assets, which he calls *asset parsimony*.

Miller also suggests that 'differentiation' can either be based on advantage from (a) product innovation or (b) marketing and branding. Mintzberg *et al.* (1995) go further in highlighting the role of price as a means of differentiating the value package offered to customers. They identify a total of six types of differentiation strategy:

- price
- image
- support
- design
- quality
- undifferentiated (or non-differentiated).

These differentiation strategies are, of course, often mixed and combined with one another. For example, the cosmetics industry, in selling perfumes, offers an interesting example of the first two strategies, *price* and *image*. The industry often reminds its critics that it is in the business of offering people an image, or identity. Particular fragrances and colours deliver particular identities at a price that is itself part of the image. Unlike standard consumer products, the industry was not prepared to compete on price. One beer brand (Stella Artois) has also promoted itself on the grounds that it is 'reassuringly expensive'.

A competitor may differentiate itself through the *support* or complementary products it provides to customers and this could take many forms: technical training, maintenance, finance, home delivery. The *quality* of the product or service also offers scope for differentiation. In Europe, washing machines from Miele, Bosch and AEG stand out from their competitors, not on features or support, but instead on the perceived *quality* and *design* of their construction. Through quality and image, they are able to command premium prices. Designer-wear, such as jeans, shirts, belts, scarves, watches, bags and other accessories with well-known brand labels, appeal to those who wish to be identified as connoisseurs of unique design.

Finally, there are many firms that get by *without differentiating* themselves in any form. Copying what the competitors are doing is an undifferentiated strategy. For some firms this is a conscious choice, but for others it is the result of managerial inability to be creative or innovative.

In addition, Mintzberg *et al.* also propose four characteristic markets, which provide a finer grain of analysis than broad or narrow focus:

- unsegmented
- segmented
- niche
- customised.

A chauffeur driven taxi service at Heathrow Airport – an example of targeting a niche market

Some firms look for an *unsegmented* mass market, others *segment* the broad market, and some target a particular *niche*. The provision of public transport exemplifies the spectrum of possibilities. At the unsegmented end of the market are the buses and trains. The market is also segmented with competitors offering taxis and different classes of air travel (club, business, first, economy). Niche markets include taxis specialising in chauffeur hire to airports or for weddings, and very discriminating and wealthy customers receive *customised* travel arrangements that can combine private jets, chauffeured limousines and escorted sightseeing or shopping.

Mintzberg's four market definitions combine with the six strategies of differentiation of the product or service to suggest a matrix of possibilities, some more likely than others. For example, a customised market strategy probably demands a customer-support differentiating strategy, while differentiating on low price and quality would normally not support a customising strategy.

Activity 3.4

Mintzberg's four characteristic markets and six strategies of product or service differentiation imply a matrix of up to 24 combination strategies. Construct a blank matrix of this type. Now review the matrix to determine whether particular strategies being followed by your own organisation can be allocated to any of the 24 locations.

Discussion

Your organisation may follow multiple strategies. In this case, perhaps you have filled in six of Mintzberg's strategy combinations. You may, however, feel that your organisation has a single well-defined strategy. If we take the example of a chauffeur hire taxi serving a niche market, it is likely that a selection of differentiation strategies may all be in place: image, quality and support (complementary services such as confirmation of flights, alliances with hotels, etc.) are all likely to be evident, although design is relatively standardised within a limited choice of brand vehicles. While price may not be an obvious source of differentiation for chauffeur hire taxis, this may depend on the density of competition in the geographic market served. If a chauffeur taxi hire company wants to win a contract for ten cars at an all-day wedding, it may well have to offer a lower price.

Finally, it is unlikely that you completed the matrix with 24 different strategies followed by your organisation. It may well be that some of the combinations seem unlikely or impossible strategies to follow in your industry. If this occurred to you as you completed the matrix, you may wish to reflect on the lessons of strategic group and strategic space analysis that you encountered in Book 3. Unlikely or impossible industry strategies can always be revisited to consider whether they could be a source of competitive innovation if conditions change.

Having discussed the various factors to be considered in formulating potential strategy options for your organisation or business unit, we will now go on to consider how managers may choose between them, and with what consequences.

4 Strategic options for products and markets, old and new

The need for a finer grain (or deeper, more detailed level) of analysis when choosing strategy extends beyond elaborating types of cost, differentiation and focus strategies. It goes beyond identifying detailed sources of advantage. Managers must be prepared to grapple with the details of how strategy will be implemented, how growth will be achieved. Embedded in the development of a strategy are many choices:

- which markets or segments to penetrate or develop
- which new or related products and services to develop
- whether to diversify or divest activities
- how best to exploit and lever existing capabilities and whether to develop new capabilities.

Some of these options are most clearly presented in the Ansoff (1965) product/market matrix shown in Figure 4.1 below.

	Product/service Present	Product/service New
Market Present	• Market penetration • Consolidation • Liquidation	• Product development
Market New	• Market development	• Diversification

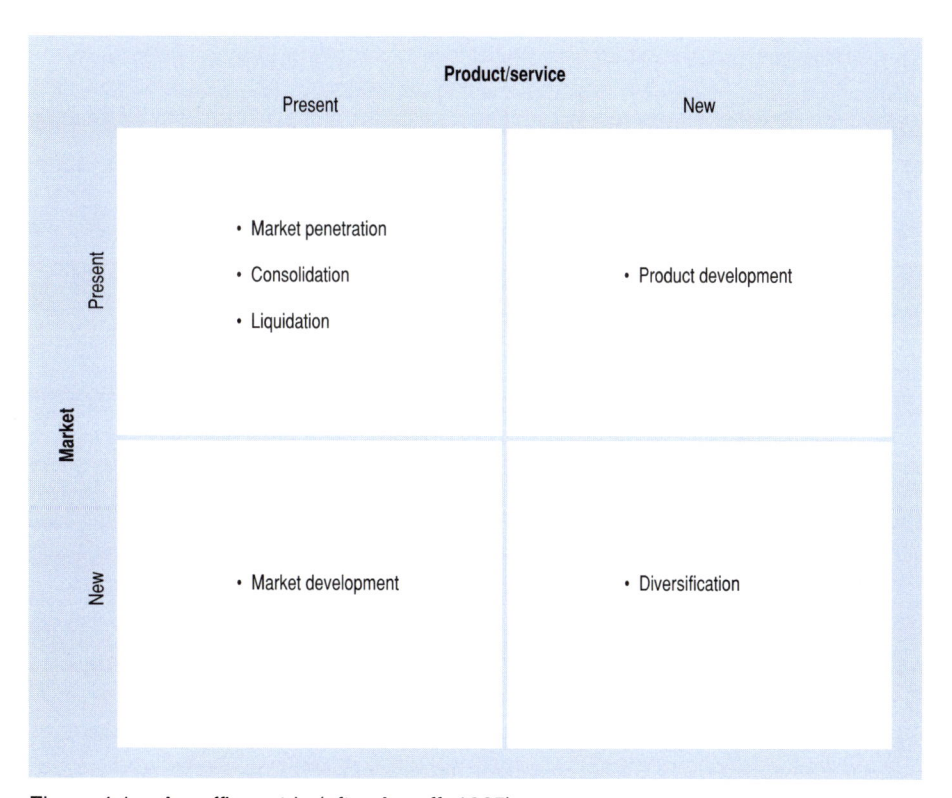

Figure 4.1　Ansoff's matrix (after Ansoff, 1965)

This matrix considers options for strategy based on two dimensions: the products or services the organisation sells and the markets it serves. In each case, it looks at the two states of 'what products and markets do we currently sell and serve' and 'which products or markets may we wish to move into in the future'. Let us consider each quadrant in turn – note that the three strategies in the upper-left quadrant are discussed individually.

4.1 PRESENT PRODUCTS, PRESENT MARKETS

4.1.1 Market penetration

A firm is pursuing a strategy of market penetration when it decides to grow its existing market share using existing products or services. The success of this strategy depends on the prospects for growth in the sector and the firm's success in exploiting competitive advantage or changing the basis of competition within the industry.

Among the alternative routes to growth, market penetration appears to carry the lowest risk. The organisation is (or should be) familiar with its products or services and with customer requirements. But there may be scope for a better understanding and for encouraging latent customer needs to emerge. The market should be able to support the generation of superior income streams from operations.

A growing market clearly invites a market penetration strategy. In contrast, in mature or static markets there will be established competitors, some of whom will be exploiting scale- or experience-based cost advantages. Successful market penetration in these conditions may depend on whether there is scope for a differentiation strategy, or whether the entrenched competitor's cost advantages can be undermined by a different and lower-cost way of competing – otherwise, a strategy to grow market share could simply result in a damaging price war. In the more extreme case where the market is in decline, and where competitors are leaving, a market penetration strategy may be an appropriate way of 'harvesting' the remaining opportunities in the sector, as we discuss more fully in Book 10.

4.1.2 Consolidation

Consolidation of competitive position requires different actions, depending on whether the market is growing, mature, or in decline.

- In growing markets, firms need to grow at least in line with the sector's growth rate. Failing to do so may result in an uncompetitive cost structure that hinders the firm's ability to invest in additional resources to improve its competitive position. Consolidation may also be necessary immediately after an acquisition or merger, since management needs time to assess how best to combine the strengths of the two entities.

- In mature markets, competitors' market shares are established and relatively stable. Competitors may seek to defend their position by increasing product or service quality, while at the same time seeking internal efficiency gains, perhaps introducing more automation to achieve cost reduction. Promotional campaigns are common ways of defending positions in relatively undifferentiated product types such as confectionery, soap powders or commodities.

- In declining markets, competitors may be liquidating their assets, while others may be acquiring those assets. Should one hold on for a turnaround in the industry's fortunes, or get out as quickly as possible? Harrigan and Porter (1983) suggest that firms in a declining industry should see it as an opportunity, and adopt an appropriate 'end-game' strategy. 'Harvesting' in such circumstances would involve maximising cash flow from existing market share by minimising new investment, cutting maintenance and promotion, reducing the product range, reducing customer support, closing down some distribution channels, and so on.

4.1.3 Liquidation

Total withdrawal from a market is referred to as liquidation because all assets are sold. It involves the closure of all activities related to that product/market territory. This option is often pursued where it has been concluded that profitability targets just cannot be met and resources would be better deployed elsewhere (or, indeed, returned to stakeholders). It may be that the market is in decline or that there has been inadequate management attention because of competing priorities. From the perspective of corporate strategy, rather than business strategy *per se*, a particular business is an asset to be bought and sold. Thus, a particular business may be divested because there are more profitable ventures elsewhere with a closer strategic 'fit' to which resources may be reallocated. The manner of divestment need not be a straightforward sale to another company. Alternative divestment routes such as management buy-outs by the existing management team were very popular during the 1980s and 1990s.

4.2 PRESENT PRODUCTS, NEW MARKETS

4.2.1 Market development

Here, the organisation takes its existing products, services and ventures into new markets. These may be defined geographically, or in terms of definable customer needs. A market development strategy may be an appropriate way of securing a foothold in a sector that is currently small or emerging, yet promises significant growth over the long term. When the firm has little influence over the development of a new sector, however, this may be a high-risk strategy.

Market development can reflect a corporate strategy rather than a business unit strategy. For example, Procter & Gamble, Unilever and Johnson & Johnson all provide a range of household cleaning products worldwide. They are credited with strong brand marketing expertise because they have worked hard at building brands as a way of differentiating their products. For these companies, market development is driven by corporate strategy, of which building global brands is a key source of product differentiation for what are essentially commodity products.

A market development strategy into new markets need not necessarily be closely related to the existing market provided there is a strategic link. A British bank's move into New Zealand, for example, might hinge on whether or not it can utilise its own expertise to help the New Zealand bank to grow, and what scope there might be to enhance its own expertise through learning how the New Zealand bank competes. This would depend, of course, on the banks' own internal capability for sharing such learning.

4.3 NEW PRODUCTS, PRESENT MARKETS

4.3.1 Product or service development

Product development can be a strategic route to growth in established markets where existing product ranges do not fully exploit the available opportunities. It can be a real source of competitive advantage to offer a complete product range, for example, as described in Mintzberg *et al.*'s (1995) differentiated strategy of 'support'. Product development is a central feature of business strategy for manufacturers of consumer electronics, such as audio-visual and kitchen appliances. In the fashion business, clothing retailers and manufacturers are usually bound to an annual cycle of anticipating fashion trends, designing, showing, manufacturing and selling them within one of two seasons – autumn/winter and spring/summer.

Customers routinely make their preferences known to the providers of products and services, and this is then used to guide product development. For example, supermarkets stock a wide range of products, partly as a result of shoppers asking for certain items. Among national supermarket chains, there are often regional differences in what is offered, reflecting variation in the ethnic mix of local populations. In other industries, product development is more accurately described as 'application' development, where competitors look for customer-specific problems and provide tailored solutions: for example, many cable manufacturing firms compete on the basis of the technical sophistication of their cabling technology, claiming low transmission loss, security from radio signal interference, physical flexibility and so on. Technical innovation may require close development work with industrial customers. For example, in producing bespoke 'umbilical cords' that allow robots to perform specialised functions in the car assembly process; or in the cable harness that runs through a car's steering column, connecting functions on the steering wheel to the car's electrical network.

Regional or local government must also remain sensitive to social trends and adapt the provision of products and services appropriately. For example, in managing local economic growth, the regional government must assess in what ways the local infrastructure is inadequate: the variety of local industries; the employment opportunities available locally; communication and transport networks; the mix of skills available within the community; and the proportion of the population of school age or unemployed. The regional government will need to consider what kinds of inward investment incentives would be appropriate for attracting which industries; what training initiatives and support services for the unemployed are most likely to help create new employment; what additional commercial accommodation, schools or housing are needed, and so on.

4.4 NEW PRODUCTS, NEW MARKETS

4.4.1 Diversification

Strategic growth through diversification can be in related or unrelated businesses. If we regard Benetton primarily as a designer and manufacturer of fashion clothing, then its ownership of some retail outlets could be regarded as a related diversification into retailing. We may also refer to this as 'forward vertical integration' because Benetton has acquired control of a business activity that lies nearer to the end user market than its core activity as a manufacturer. In contrast, a firm may choose to 'integrate backwards' towards the raw material or other supply inputs that go into making its own products. Finally, if the firm acquires a provider of complementary products or services, this is referred to as 'horizontal integration', as when an accounting firm acquires a legal practice and begins to offer legal advice; or an advertising agency acquires a public relations firm, or an airline acquires a chain of travel agents to sell complete holidays.

There are many reasons why a firm may choose to diversify, including the opportunity to reduce input costs by finding and controlling a new source of raw materials, or by controlling a unique resource, perhaps a design consultancy. Horizontal integration of otherwise independent businesses can lead to a combined value that is greater than the sum of the parts – the effect known as 'synergy' (which we will discuss at greater length in Book 11). Another reason for diversification might be that the firm sees the industry that it is currently in as a declining one, or one where it can no longer make superior returns. Occasionally, firms make a scientific discovery that has no apparent use in the existing product market and actively look for potential new applications.

A strategy of diversification for a public or voluntary organisation may, for example, focus on alternative sources of resource acquisition to enhance or expand service delivery. This is well established in higher education, although the idea of universities appealing on a charitable basis for resources is not always well accepted by the service receivers (such as undergraduate students) who may feel that central government should provide the resource. However, the principle of private endowments for some professional posts or specific research projects is very common.

Diversification clearly carries significant risk and uncertainty, and Biggadike (1979) found that diversification took an average of eight years to show a positive net income stream. Often the strategic thinking behind an acquisition is muddled and unsound, and only partly supported by internal or external data. Many acquired diversifications never show a positive return on investment and are subsequently divested.

4.5 EXAMPLE: NEW AND OLD IN RETAIL BANKING

We can now illustrate the discussion up to this point in Section 4 by applying the Ansoff product/market matrix to a specific example: the strategies of a typical commercial retail bank. Faced with a choice as to how to grow its business, it may choose to pursue all six of Ansoff's strategies for products and markets:

- *Market penetration* – may involve the opening of new branches in areas of lower customer penetration, or promotional initiatives to attract key new customers (e.g. students or teenagers or high net-worth private clients).
- *Consolidation* – may mean the introduction of customer databases and information automation to process queries and transactions faster and more accurately.

- *Liquidation* – might involve the sale or closure of branches in depressed areas or geographic regions where a critical mass of customers cannot be achieved.
- *Market development* – could mean the bank opening branches in overseas markets where none currently exist, because growth prospects in those markets are more attractive or synergies can be achieved in services sold to international customers.
- *Product development* – may involve the bank in offering telephone banking. Although the core features of telephone banking may be similar to branch banking, it does offer a development of product for customers in its convenience and flexibility (for example with 24-hour operation).
- *Diversification* – might mean the bank sets up a direct-sell telephone-based insurance company, selling or acquiring car or home insurance with no reference to the bank's existing branch network.

If we were to map these strategies onto Ansoff's matrix, the following would result:

	Product/service Present	**New**
Market Present	Market penetration • open new branches Consolidation • information automation Liquidation • close branches	Product development • offer telephone banking
New	Market development • open overseas branches	Diversification • set up direct sales insurance company

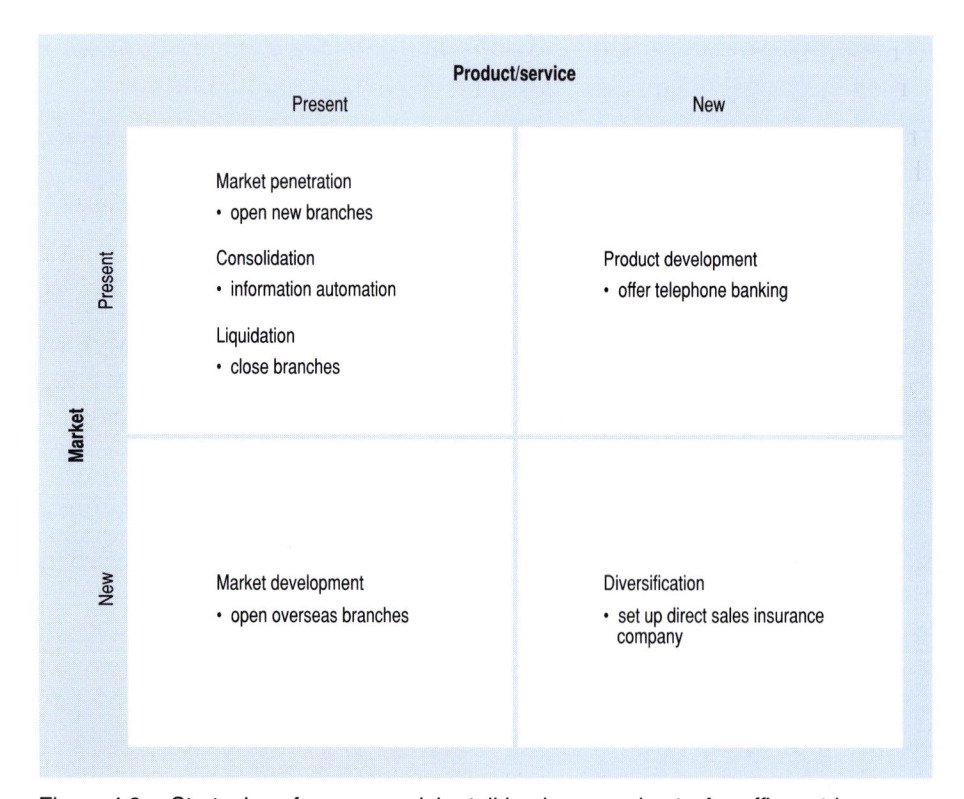

Figure 4.2   Strategies of a commercial retail bank mapped onto Ansoff's matrix

4.6 BOUNDARIES AND THE CHOICES BETWEEN OLD AND NEW

The Ansoff matrix provides us with a useful way of further selecting suitable product and market strategies, in support of generic strategies, to exploit an organisation's sources of advantage. It reinforces the point that competitive strategies cannot simply be made at an abstract, generic level. The implementation of that strategy at the product/market level must also be considered.

It is, however, important to realise that this level of detailed analysis in choosing strategy goes beyond simply considering the two dimensions of products and markets. A host of other choices must be made. For example, does our strategy require us to acquire new resources or strategic assets, or can the strategy be developed by exploiting those we already have? Book 4 identified the importance of distinctive capabilities, routines and skills as sources of advantage. Must these be developed or acquired anew, or do we intend to leverage our existing sources of advantage in new markets? Do we have to develop entirely new or amended technologies to operate our new strategy? An organisation may be faced with the inevitability of changing its capabilities, resources or technologies if it is to develop entirely new sources of advantage or alter an apparently stable industry structure for its own benefit.

These choices between pursuing a strategy in old or new markets, using old or new products, resources, capabilities or technologies, also raise a related set of questions discussed in Book 4. Does the organisation attempt to own the resources itself or merely obtain access to them? Can other organisations provide the skills and capabilities more effectively? Does the organisation try to replicate, initiate or license a proprietary technology? Does it rely on agents or partners to provide sales cover in some markets (as Glaxo did with Zantac)?

These are questions about the boundaries of the organisation. They imply choices about whether an organisation acquires assets, resources or capabilities (or even entire companies) or develops them internally. This is the 'make or buy' decision discussed in Book 4 when transaction cost economics were considered. The obverse of a decision to acquire or develop internally might equally be the outsourcing dilemma: retain or divest? Such boundary questions cannot be limited, however, to make or buy decisions. Increasingly, organisations are seeking access to resources and capabilities through devices such as joint ventures and collaborative networks. The benefits of relational and classical contracting discussed in Book 2 are important to these types of decisions. Further, in joint ventures and collaborative networks, the boundaries of the organisation are no longer clear-cut (if they ever were). Decisions must then be made about how these boundaries, networks and ventures are managed.

These topics, discussed in part in Books 2 and 4, will also be covered in Books 10 and 11, but you should be aware at present that they are all important strategic decisions about the fine grain of strategy, necessary to its successful formulation and implementation.

5 Testing strategic options and strategic choices

5.1 Introduction

We have discussed the importance of identifying an organisation's sources of advantage as having key importance in choosing strategy. We have also considered generic ways of classifying strategies to exploit those sources of advantage, and the need for a more detailed level of analysis and choice if strategies are to be implemented successfully. Choices about which segments to target, which markets to enter, what products to produce, what resources and capabilities to develop, whether to develop strategies alone or in alliance and so on, are all important to strategic success. We will next consider how we might evaluate strategic options that are open to us.

5.2 The tests of suitability, feasibility and acceptability

Johnson and Scholes (1988) suggest three sets of generic testing criteria: suitability, feasibility and acceptability.

Suitability

The *suitability* of a proposed strategy can be assessed by the extent to which it matches the needs identified from a strategic analysis. Such a test of suitability is sometimes regarded as a test of consistency with the environmental or resource analyses and their fit with the organisational objectives.

- Obviously, the proposed strategy should address the strategic problem or opportunity identified in the strategic analysis. Does it overcome an identified resource weakness or environmental threat?
- Next, the strategy should capitalise on the organisation's identified resources and capabilities and the way they relate to external opportunities.
- Finally, the strategy should fit the organisation's objectives, such as required rates of return on capital, profitability measures and other, non-financial, performance indicators.

Feasibility

The test of *feasibility* of a proposed strategy will consider how well it would work in practice and how difficult it might be to achieve. The questions to be asked would include:
- Can the strategy be resourced? Even the most brilliant strategy cannot be implemented if, for example, the organisation's financial position is too weak to raise capital.

- Can the organisation actually achieve the required level of operational performance, say in quality and service levels? Would a strategy aimed at reducing costs in manufacturing run into problems associated with inadequate managerial resource, insufficient numbers of trained staff, or inadequate process and product technologies?
- How will the competition react and how will the organisation cope with that reaction? For example, a strategy to increase market share by reducing prices may lead to fierce competitive reaction.

In considering the feasibility of a strategy, however, there is a danger of ignoring the challenge of strategic stretch and leverage (Prahalad and Hamel, 1994) discussed in Book 1. Feasibility should therefore reflect the challenge as well as the test of ambition.

Acceptability

Johnson and Scholes' final evaluation criterion is *acceptability*. This addresses the issues of how stakeholders might feel about the expected outcomes of the strategy – typically in terms of risk, profitability, reward, ethics and the effect on relationships. Meeting reasonable stakeholder expectations is clearly a crucial test for acceptability in a strategy. Test questions include:

- What will be the financial or cost–benefit performance? Is there an unacceptable risk of endangering overall liquidity or affecting capital structure?
- Is there a risk that the organisation's relationships with its stakeholders could be unacceptably affected? Is the proposal likely to alienate employees, institutional shareholders, existing customers or clients, or governmental organisations?
- What is the effect of the proposed strategy on the internal systems and procedures? Even if feasible, will there be additional strain on staff?

The three tests of suitability, feasibility and acceptability provide an initial set of screening tools for strategic choice. They prompt managers to be explicit about the underlying rationale behind proposed strategies and to assess the associated risks and uncertainties. The criteria also guide the softer process of assessing how acceptable the proposed strategies might be to stakeholders.

5.3 THE TESTS OF CONSISTENCY, CONSONANCE, ADVANTAGE AND FEASIBILITY

It is usually helpful to test proposed strategies from a number of perspectives. Rumelt (1995) suggests the four tests of 'consistency, consonance, advantage and feasibility'. He acknowledges that it may be impossible to demonstrate conclusively that a particular business strategy can, or will, work, let alone be an optimal strategy. He points out, however, that all proposed strategies can be tested for four types of critical flaws. As will be seen, there is some overlap with the criteria of Johnson and Scholes.

Consistency

Rumelt suggests a *consistency* test: the proposed strategy must not present mutually inconsistent goals and policies. You may feel that failing this test is unlikely, but it may be a particularly necessary test for emergent strategies since these will not have been explicitly formulated and may have formed over time in an *ad hoc* fashion. Even deliberate strategies may contain compromise arrangements between power groups.

Inconsistency in strategy is not simply a flaw in logic. A key function of strategy is to provide a coherent framework for organisational action. Rumelt cites the practical example of high-technology firms that face a strategic choice between offering customised high-cost products and standardised low-cost products. If senior management does not enunciate a clear and consistent view of where the firm stands on these issues, there will be continuing conflict between sales, design, engineering and manufacturing people. The same situation might arise in a public-sector organisation where specialised interests conflict with general goals and where priorities in allocation of resources are difficult: for example, which medical treatments should be publicly funded, or whether pre-school, primary or secondary education should be allocated additional available funds.

Rumelt then goes on to argue that an organisation relates to its environment in two main aspects:

1. It must match and be adapted to the environment – the products or services must create more value than they cost.
2. It must compete with other organisations that are also trying to adapt and prosper.

Consonance

Rumelt therefore proposes a test of *consonance* that focuses on the creation of social value: to evaluate the economic relationships that characterise the business and determine whether or not sufficient value is being created to sustain the demand for the strategy in the long term.

The major difficulty in evaluating consonance is that most of the critical threats or substitutes that come from the external environment will also threaten the whole industry. Management may be so focused on existing competition that the threat is only recognised after the damage is done. Rumelt also points out that many forecasting techniques do not reveal potentially critical changes that arise from *interaction* among combinations of trends. For example, supermarkets came into being only when home refrigeration allowed shoppers to buy in bulk. Similarly, retail parks depend on an increase in car ownership. The key to the test of consonance is to grasp why the organisation exists and the basic economic foundation that supports and defines the business, and then to study the consequences of key changes.

Advantage

Rumelt's third test is about competitive *advantage* or whether the organisation can capture enough of the value it creates. As you learned in Book 4, competitive strategy is the art of creating and exploiting those advantages that are most telling, enduring and most difficult to duplicate. The strategy must provide for the creation and/or maintenance of a competitive advantage in one or more of three roots:

- superior skills

- superior resources
- superior position.

Feasibility

Rumelt's final test of strategy is *feasibility*. This was discussed in Section 5.2 and we do not need to repeat it here.

5.4 TESTING FOR EFFICIENCY, EFFECTIVENESS, ECONOMY AND EQUITY

Public and private not-for-profit organisations may often choose to test proposed strategies against objectives which are founded on the 'four Es': efficiency, effectiveness, economy and equity.

There can be conflicting objectives if, for example, both efficiency and equity are to be served. By its nature, equitable service distribution has a tendency to be economically inefficient. For example, the cost of granting planning permission for a building or an extension can vary widely, depending on the nature of the property. Despite this, a standard charge is usually made, so that low-cost permissions effectively subsidise high-cost ones. In the same way, the environmental health department of a local government organisation may wish to keep domestic cleansing costs down by collecting every two weeks, instead of once or even twice a week. This could be in a conflict with a parallel objective of, say, reducing rat populations or presenting a pleasant appearance for tourists.

Activity 5.1

Grant (1995, p. 26) describes four critical elements that he thinks should feature in a successfully formulated strategy, which can be summarised as:

- goals that are simple, consistent and long-term
- a profound understanding of the competitive environment
- an objective appraisal of resources
- effective implementation.

Test your own organisation against these elements. Does your organisation have all four elements of these tests of a successful strategy? If not, do you still consider your organisation's strategy successful? Are there any further critical elements for successful strategy formulation that you have identified?

5.5 RISK AND UNCERTAINTY IN STRATEGIC CHOICE

Strategy is about charting a course for the future: will governments alter legislation? How will competitors react? Will war break out in one of the countries where business is carried out? Strategic choice must always be made in the face of such risk and uncertainty. You should be well aware of the difference between risk and uncertainty.

Risk is concerned with assessing the probability of foreseen outcomes.

In contrast, *uncertainty* is to do with outcomes that may be unforeseen, or those which are foreseen but against which a degree of estimated risk cannot be set.

Running a successful ice-cream vending operation demands a careful assessment of elements of risk and uncertainty

For example, suppose you are offered the chance to buy an ice-cream van for £5,000. If the weather is good, historical records show that you will make a return on capital employed of 20 per cent; if fair, 15 per cent; if poor, around 5 per cent. You also know that there is a 30 per cent chance of the weather being good, 60 per cent fair and 10 per cent poor – based again on historical records. You are now in a position to assess three trading scenarios and assign a probability to each. In contrast, some very unpredictable event could occur, for example you may discover that the ice-cream van you have bought provides the security on the previous owner's loan; it cannot be legally sold and you must return it! This is a situation of *uncertainty* and you cannot ascribe it a probability. For a second example, a new film carries the *risk* of loss if cinemas are less than 50 per cent full – the break-even point. However, there is always the unpredictable *uncertainty* that the film fails to gain a cinematic release (although video release may recoup some of the loss).

Assessing uncertainties and weighing up risks is a difficult, often personal, process and very dependent on the business environment. In making choices about strategy, acceptance of different degrees of risk is often a matter of an individual manager's (or group of managers') personal preferences. Some individuals are very risk-averse, others take risks almost as a matter of routine. In fact, Wilde (1982) suggests that:

- tolerance to risk affects the way in which people assess information
- people behave so as to maintain a certain level of subjective risk at all times.

For example, in countries where the wearing of seat-belts in cars is compulsory by law, drivers appear to adjust their average driving speeds upwards, merely re-creating the previous risk/safety ratio.

Strategic risks that would be acceptable in one industry, such as PC manufacture, would be quite unacceptable in another, such as health care or aerospace. Quinn (1978) feels that perceived risk is largely a function of an individual's knowledge about a sector or industry. This raises the question as to whether managers entering new industries are best equipped to assess the risks and uncertainties of it. For example, would managers used to predicting stable revenues in public monopoly utilities be best placed to identify the risks and uncertainties of, say, software design and manufacture.

There are modelling techniques available which may *help* managers to make these judgements, but it is important to note that strategy can rarely be *optimised* in this way, as the variables are usually too complex. You have to use your judgement to determine the optimum strategy.

Judgement may involve 'satisficing' and compromise. For example, in most organisations there will be a drive to attain the lowest possible cost, in order to yield the highest possible added-value. Alternatively, the strategic intent might be to maximise market share without regard (within limits) for the cost. You will appreciate that there may well be trade-offs in the face of conflicting objectives, some of which will be measurable, as with finance or market share, and other objectives will be expressions of stakeholder preference. Measurement of success in strategic situations is frequently concerned with reaching the most acceptable solution in the face of conflicting objectives, inadequate resources, or unfavourable attitudes.

5.6 FUTURE MODELLING AND SCENARIO PLANNING

Although strategic optimisation can rarely be achieved through modelling, it can be valuable to use future modelling and risk management techniques, such as scenario planning. Read the following passage, which is adapted from Tapiero (1988).

> Future modelling is a basic activity which consists of transforming a set of possible and future-oriented events into a coherent whole. This is complicated, because it requires a very clear understanding of the causes of change; that is, we seek to establish not only causal links between events, but how these links are maintained over time. In planning, we face an unmanageable number (indeed an unlimited number) of possible futures. Therefore, if we are to make a reproduction of the future in the present, we must determine a substitute for it.
>
> This substitute is not what will necessarily occur; it is our guess about what may occur. When managers' intentions are combined with such guesses about the future, then we engage in learning, adaptation and, more generally, in uncertainty reduction, i.e. we replace a string of unknown events by another (or the same) string of events with an altered likelihood of occurrence. In this manner, managers seek to influence and possibly control the risks of the environment within which they function. This is called risk management.

> Whenever a model for the future and a reduction of uncertainty has been achieved, alternative courses of action can be tested for their future impact. By manipulating the model on the basis of credible assumptions, we obtain credible time paths of the variables with which we are most directly concerned. [...] Managers' intentions are combined with such guesses about the future in an information-gathering, learning and adaptation process. The plans are then adjusted as necessary to achieve the desired risk–return ratio.
>
> Planning in this sense is at the core of a great many managerial activities. To render relevant choices more manageable and to gain more information concerning the impact of an action upon the future, we need information.

Tapiero describes a rational approach to risk management and future modelling. He emphasises the management intention, not to forecast the future, but to estimate the range of outcomes and their associated probabilities.

It is also important not to confuse the basic risk inherent in any strategic option with strategic options that are designed to reduce risk. For example, when an organisation enters a new market or launches a new product, it might adopt a strategy that is perceived as low-risk, such as the use of joint ventures or licensing of technology. Here, one of the strategic intentions is to reduce risk. Of course, the decision still carries with it a basic risk.

Capabilities in systematic risk management may, indeed, be at the very heart of some businesses, for example life assurance, liability insurance or market-making in futures exchanges. Other companies may benefit from access to superior skills in the routine management of future risks and uncertainties, for example hedging foreign currency realisations.

Future modelling capabilities such as scenario planning can also give some organisations an advantage in dealing with uncertain but rapid or discontinuous change. For example, scenario planning has been pioneered and developed by the oil company, Shell (de Geus, 1988). In February 1986, the price of crude oil collapsed from $27 per barrel to $8 at its lowest, before settling back at a range of between $13 and $19 for the next ten years. This was an unimaginable catastrophe in the industry. Two years earlier, however, Shell executives were asked to consider the impact of a $10 price on the company. Initially incredulous, the executives had, however, settled back to produce plans of how the company would survive. These scenario plans are widely credited with giving Shell an advantage in reacting quickly and effectively to the price collapse.

5.7 RISK, REWARD AND SUPERIOR PROFITABILITY

Strategic choice should take into account the risks associated with different strategic options. These risks may not be quantifiable but they can normally be categorised into high, medium or low. (You may have met risk projection in earlier studies in the use of the capital–asset pricing model, in which the riskiness of corporate activity is related to the pricing of an organisation's shares and, thus, the financial rewards of shareholding.)

The whole issue of stakeholder objectives (as discussed in Book 2) and their attitudes to risk–return relationships, sets the context in which strategic choice has to take place. One way of characterising the different financial goals of different stakeholders, and the different financial rating with which they will be primarily concerned, is set out in Figures 5.1 and 5.2. The purpose of these figures is not to debate the precise location of different stakeholder groups (which *is* clearly a matter of debate), but to understand the implications of trade-offs between risk and return.

Clearly, in the real world there is a relationship between risk and return – other things being equal, people will demand higher returns from more risky investments of resources. Thus the pattern of expected normal returns runs from the top left-hand corner of the matrix to the bottom right. This does not, however, stop stakeholders seeking to further maximise their returns while minimising their risks. This is why the stakeholders on the matrix are not distributed evenly along a straight line (Figure 5.1). The concerns of the different stakeholders will, in turn, lead them to place emphasis on different measures of financial performance (Figure 5.2).

Day (1990) argues that such financial reward evaluation of strategic choice will be credible only if stakeholders address three fundamental issues that determine the pay-off from a strategic choice:

- the prospects for superior profitability
- the chances that superior profitability will be realised
- the acceptability of the risk–reward ratio.

These three issues are discussed in turn below.

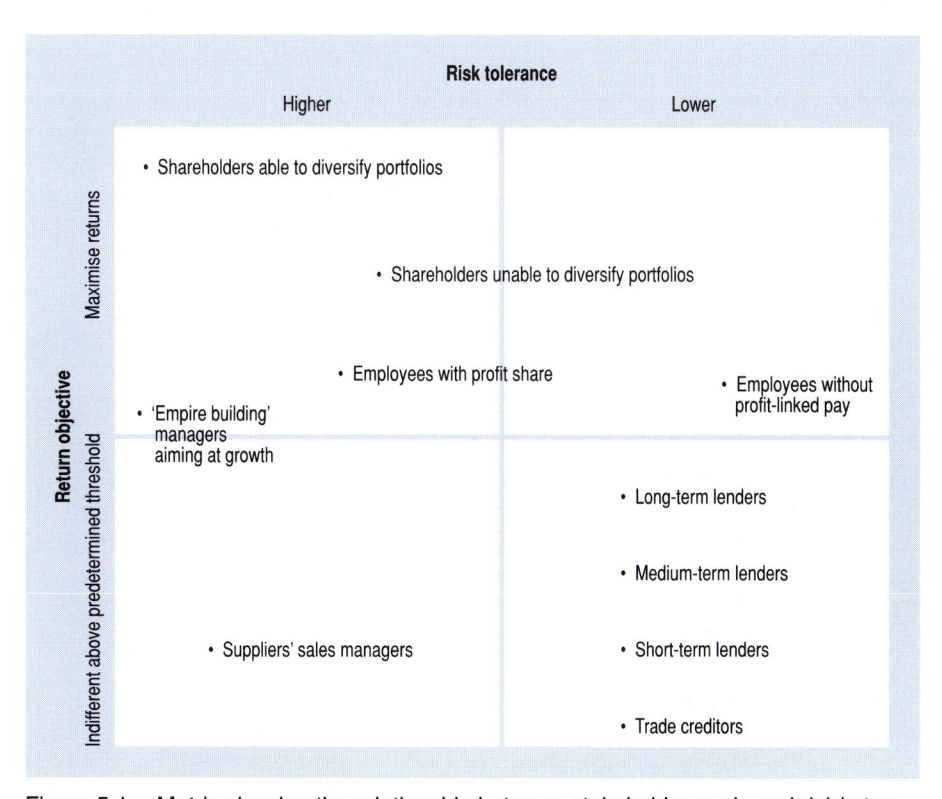

Figure 5.1 Matrix showing the relationship between stakeholder goals and risk/return

	Risk tolerance	
	Higher	Lower
Maximise returns	• High return on equity • High leverage acceptable • High turnover growth aim • Fixed cost bias in corporate costs	• High return on total capital • High leverage unacceptable • Lower turnover growth to avoid cash problems • Prefer variable cost bias
Indifferent above predetermined threshold	• Growth in turnover • Growth in asset base • High leverage acceptable	• Low growth • Low leverage • High quick ratio • High current ratio • Stable markets

Return objective (vertical axis label)

Figure 5.2   Effect of risk/return attitudes on ratios

In this course, you have encountered two main views of how *the prospects for superior profitability* can be assessed. Superior profits can be achieved:

1. relative to organisations in other industries, by entering an attractive industry or by altering the structure of an industry to make it more attractive
2. relative to firms in the same industry, by achieving and sustaining a competitive advantage based on distinctive resources and capabilities.

In practice, the strategic choices facing most managers pursuing superior profits will tend to focus on improving profits by achieving competitive advantage. These choices can be related to the tests of consonance (the creation of 'social value') and advantage proposed by Rumelt in Section 5.3. This is because the combined effect of exit barriers from the existing industry or sector, and entry barriers into the new industry or sector, usually make such movements unrealistic.

The chances that superior profitability will be achieved is the second of Day's fundamental issues. Given that the opportunity promises superior profits, what chance does the intended strategy have of being realised? Does the organisation have the skills and necessary resources or, if not, can the deficiencies be overcome without too much cost or delay? If the superior profits derive from a competitive advantage, is this sustainable? These concerns are clearly related to Rumelt's test of feasibility in Section 5.3. Feasibility considerations are also related to the overall uncertainty of the project and are not to be confused with risk.

The third of Day's fundamental issues is *the acceptability of the risk–reward ratio* as discussed in Section 5.7. The importance of relating investment risk–return profiles and trade-offs back to the objectives and risk–return profiles of stakeholders, demonstrates again the relationship between Day's focus on risk–reward ratios and both Johnson and Scholes's acceptability test (Section 5.2) and Rumelt's consistency test (Section 5.3).

6 Summary and Conclusion

This book has concentrated on choice in strategy and identified a number of tests of options and criteria which will help an organisation choose an appropriate and successful strategy. In particular, the importance of strategy as a means of exploiting sources of advantage has been affirmed as a key consideration in strategic choice.

The book deliberately avoids discussion of the organisational and social processes by which strategic choices are made, as these issues are dealt with in Book 7. Choices in strategy could, for example, be made using a 'linear' planning approach such as the model proposed by Andrews discussed in Book 1. It is quite possible to take the ideas the course has discussed so far and map them on to Andrews' model, as shown in Table 6.1:

Table 6.1 Strategy formulation using Andrews' corporate planning process

Andrews' stage	Where discussed
• identification of organisational objectives	Book 2
• appraisal of the external and internal environment	Books 3 and 4
• formulation of several alternative strategies	Book 5
• evaluation of these alternative strategies against objectives and in the context of resources available and management values; followed by strategy selection	Book 5
• implementation of chosen strategy	throughout the course

Book 1 also pointed out, however, that analysing or formulating strategy is likely to be an iterative process, in which actions can occur simultaneously and without the explicit intention of the organisation and its management. Mintzberg (1994) has categorised academic schools of thought on how strategy is made and strategic choices taken. He noted two main categories of perspective that seek to explain the same observable personal and organisational behaviours of strategy process.

1 *Prescriptive* – seeking to prescribe the ways of making choices about strategy. It attempts to define, through a rational process, what should happen in strategy.

2 *Descriptive* – seeking to describe the organisational strategy-making process; this rationalisation is done with hindsight after strategy has been made. It explains strategy 'as it is rather than how it should be'.

Ohmae (1984) has written persuasively about the boundary between the rational *prescriptive* approach to making strategy and the *descriptive* approach. Synthesising successful business strategies never results just from rigorous analysis, but from a particular state of mind. Insight and a drive for achievement fuel a thought process that is creative and intuitive rather than rational. Ohmae acknowledges the role of analysis; indeed, strategists could hardly do without it, but they use it to stimulate the creative process, test the resulting ideas and ensure successful execution of high-potential 'wild' ideas. No matter how difficult or unprecedented the problem, a breakthrough to the best possible solution can come only from a combination of rational analysis (based on the real nature of things and imaginative reintegration of all the different items into a new pattern), and by the exercising of individual thought and judgement. Ohmae believes that great strategies, like great works of art or great scientific discoveries, although they all call for technical mastery in the analysis, must originate in insights and judgements that are beyond the reach of conscious analysis.

As a student of strategy, you will encounter both prescriptive and descriptive accounts of how choices are or can be made in strategy. You need to be flexible enough to recognise the elements and the merits of both approaches and be prepared to advance your own individual thoughts.

REFERENCES

Ansoff, H.I. (1965) *Corporate Strategy*, McGraw-Hill, New York.

Biggadike, R. (1979) 'The risky business of diversification', *Harvard Business Review*, May/June.

Bowman, C. and Asch, D. (1996) *Managing Strategy*, Macmillan, Basingstoke.

Day, G.S. (1990) *Market-driven Strategy Process for Creating Value*, The Free Press, New York.

de Geus, A. (1988) 'Planning as learning', *Harvard Business Review*, March–April.

Grant, R. (1995) *Contemporary Strategy Analysis* (2nd ed.), Blackwell, Oxford.

Harrigan, K.R. and Porter, M.E. (1983) 'End-game strategies for declining industries', *Harvard Business Review*, July/August.

Jarillo, J-C. and Martinez, J.I. under the direction of Stevenson, H.H. (1988) 'Benetton SpA', Harvard Business School Case 9-389-074.

Johnson, G. and Scholes, K. (1988) *Exploring Corporate Strategy* (2nd ed.), Prentice-Hall, Hemel Hempstead.

Kay, J. (1993) *Foundations of Corporate Success*, Oxford University Press, Oxford.

Miller, D. (1986) 'Configurations of strategy and structure: towards a synthesis', in Asch, D. and Bowman, C. (eds) *Readings in Strategic Management*, Macmillan, Basingstoke.

Mintzberg, H., Quinn, B.J. and Ghoshal, S. (1995) *The Strategy Process*, Prentice-Hall, Hemel Hempstead.

Mintzberg, H. (1994) *The Rise and Fall of Strategic Planning*, Prentice-Hall, Hemel Hempstead.

Ohmae, K. (1983) *The Mind of the Strategist*, Penguin, Harmondsworth.

Porter, M.E. (1980) *Competitive Strategy*, The Free Press, New York.

Porter, M.E. (1985) *Competitive Advantage*, The Free Press, New York.

Prahalad, C.K. and Hamel, G. (1994) 'New strategy paradigms', *Strategic Management Journal*, Vol. 15, Special Issue.

Quinn, J.B. (1978) 'Strategic change: logical incrementalism', *Sloan Management Review*, Vol. 1, p. 20.

Rumelt, R. (1995) 'The evaluation of business strategy', in Mintzberg, H., Quinn, B.J. and Ghoshal, S., *op. cit.*

Smith, R.J. (1994) *Strategic Planning and Management in the Public Sector*, Longman, London.

Tapiero, C. (1988) *Applied Stochastic Models and Control in Management*, North-Holland, Amsterdam.

Wilde, G.J.S. (1982) 'The theory of risk homeostasis', *Risk Analysis*, Vol. 2, No. 4, pp. 209–225.

Acknowledgements

Grateful acknowledgement is made to the following sources for permission to reproduce material in this book:

Photographs

Page 16: © Lada Cars; *page 17:* © Porsche Cars GB Ltd; *page 19:* (Rover 618) © Rover Group; *page 19:* (Honda Accord) © Honda Motor Europe Ltd; *page 23:* courtesy of Tristar Cars; *page 26:* Mike Levers/Open University.

Figures

Figure 3.1: Porter, M. E. 1985, *Competitive Advantage: Creating and Sustaining Superior Performance*, p. 12, figure 1.3, Simon & Schuster; *Figure 4.1:* Ansoff, H. I. 1968, *Corporate Strategy*, Table 6.1, McGraw-Hill © 1968 H. Igor Ansoff.

BOOK 6

STRATEGY AND INNOVATION

Author: Paul Quintas

MBA

Strategy

Contents

1 Introduction — 5
   1.1 The idea of innovation — 5
   1.2 Learning objectives of this book — 8
   1.3 Shape, scope and content of this book — 9

2 Frameworks for understanding innovation — 10
   2.1 Innovation and macro-environmental change — 10
   2.2 An innovation typology — 15
   2.3 Process innovation — 17
   2.4 Product and process interdependence — 19
   2.5 Diffusion of innovations — 20

3 Innovation and strategy — 22
   3.1 Creating advantage through innovation — 23
   3.2 The drivers of innovation — 24
   3.3 Technology-push or market-pull? — 28
   3.4 Investment in innovation — 32
   3.5 Strategic options — 34
   3.6 Key innovation success factors — 36

4 Innovation in context — 38
   4.1 Innovation and the service sector — 38
   4.2 Large firms, small firms and innovation — 41
   4.3 Innovation in mature industries — 44

5 Building the capability to innovate — 46
   5.1 Innovation and organisational capability — 46
   5.2 Innovation and organisation — 47
   5.3 Innovation as knowledge management — 49
   5.4 Strategic collaboration and innovation — 50
   5.5 Organisations and individuals — 52

6 Summary and conclusion — 54

References — 56

Acknowledgements — 60

1 INTRODUCTION

He that will not apply new remedies must expect new evils, for time is the greatest innovator.

(Francis Bacon)

1.1 THE IDEA OF INNOVATION

Strategy is concerned with creating the capability to innovate, and with appropriating and sustaining the advantage from innovation.

This book focuses on innovation as a central component of strategic management. The competitive advantage of individual firms, the capability of public-sector and not-for-profit organisations to continue to satisfy the needs of their client groups, and the ability of national economies to prosper, depend to a very great extent on innovation. By *innovation* we mean the development and bringing to market, or into effective use, of new or significantly improved products, processes, services and systems.

More than this rather basic definition, innovation is the expression of knowledge and creativity in tangible form – it is the result of human intelligence brought to bear on some practical problem in a given context. Innovation, therefore, results from organisational and inter-organisational human-centred processes which must be managed:

> The innovation process begins with a mandate which must be set at the highest levels of the corporation by identifying goals and priorities and once identified, these must be communicated all the way down the line.
>
> *(Akio Morita, Chairman of Sony Corporation, First UK Innovation Lecture, Royal Society, 16 February 1992)*

This book is not about *technology per se*, if we define technology as meaning devices, materials, artefacts and tools. The history of innovation also includes many examples of how technical organisational changes have transformed our working lives. This includes the factory system, an organisational innovation which pre-dates the introduction of that technological icon of the industrial revolution, the steam engine. More recently, just-in-time (JIT) and total quality management (TQM) represent organisational innovations that *can* be introduced without the accompaniment of new technologies.

However, the history of human civilisation, for good or evil, is also the history of technology, from the earliest use of flint tools and the plough to Semtex explosive and the World Wide Web. Whilst acknowledging the importance of non-technical innovation, we also must recognise the *interdependence* of technology and organisation.

In his seminal work *Technics and Civilisation* (1934), Lewis Mumford identified the mechanical clock as the most important technology of western civilisation. When clocks became widespread and the hours and minutes precisely and continuously measured, people's lives began to be ordered according to this artificial representation of time rather than the traditional rhythms of life. This profound shift eventually made possible the factory system, and later the assembly line, time-and-motion study, and now 24-hour trading. This does not mean that these radical innovations were shaped and determined by the clock – they are all examples of innovations resulting from the interaction of social, economic, technological and political factors. This illustrates once again Fahey and Narayanan's (1986) argument (discussed in Book 3) that the macro-environment can only be properly understood as an interrelated system.

In this book we therefore address both technological and organisational innovation, although the emphasis is on the former. Books 7, 8 and 9 will place greater emphasis on capabilities for organisational change.

Technology is a complex and comprehensive concept encompassing not just physical hardware and tools, but also a body of knowledge about technique. Technology is thus about techniques, methods and activities which include cumulative and experiential knowledge. This is particularly relevant to our later discussions on the sources of knowledge that results in innovation.

Innovation has become a safe and acceptable thing for managers to advocate. However, innovation in reality may be a less than comfortable phenomenon. It can be unpredictable, high risk, hard to manage and even harder to achieve successfully. For every Sony Walkman there are very many failures, and it is clear that amongst the multitude of reasons for innovation failure, managerial factors, rather than technical issues, are what most need addressing to improve innovative performance.

Innovation can be intensely destabilising within product markets, industrial sectors, and indeed national and international economies. While your own organisation may be striving to innovate to improve your *existing* products and services, others in the competitive environment (who may come from a different sector of the economy) may develop radically innovative products or services that negate your achievements.

For example, in the 1970s National Cash Register (NCR) failed to respond to the fact that micro-electronics technology was transforming its market (Foster, 1986). Astonishingly, over a period of just four years, 80 per cent of the US cash register market went from electromechanical to electronic technology (see Figure 1.1). Twenty thousand out of 90,000 NCR jobs were lost, and the company had to write off $140 million of new electromechanical equipment. *Fortune* magazine later noted: 'NCR was still clinging to the past, endlessly refining an obsolete electromechanical technology, even though the computer revolution was on the verge of overwhelming it' (Seneker, as quoted in Steward (1994)).

Here we find our first conundrum in the innovation paradox. NCR and other examples of technology-induced destabilisation suggest that the last strategy an organisation should adopt is focused, incremental development of their products and processes. If you do this, the NCR example says, significant innovations from entirely new entrants with radically new products will wipe yours from the catalogues and the distribution channels. However, research into successful innovation emphasises that organisations do need to cumulatively build the capability to innovate, and that companies tend to innovate in their existing product markets and areas of expertise (Pavitt, 1991). It is evident that the success of Japanese manufacturing industry in the post-war period is largely based on meticulous attention to *incremental* process and product innovation (Womack *et al.*, 1990).

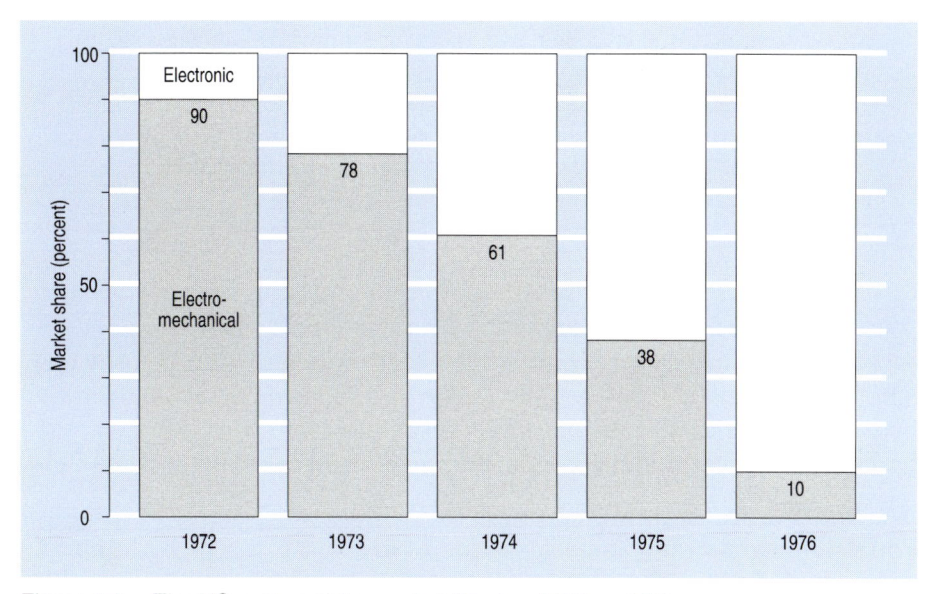

Figure 1.1   The US cash register market (Foster, 1986, p. 141)

So the challenge is to develop strategies that enable your organisation to do both: to build and nurture the capability to innovate in specific areas, while at the same time being aware of, and able to take advantage of, technological innovations and other developments from outside your organisation. This requires a dynamic approach to strategy, technology and organisation.

Innovation is of strategic interest for two principal reasons:
1   as a threat to organisations supplying existing products and services
2   as a source of strategic advantage for innovating organisations.

We aim to address both these aspects of innovation. We begin by placing innovation at the centre of large-scale economic changes that affect the organisation's environment, and to which strategic responses must be made. We then examine the strategic issues that affect the ability of organisations themselves to innovate. They may innovate in many ways:

- new products, systems or services
- organisational innovation
- internal process innovation incorporating external innovations, for example using a new machine tool or a computer network
- innovations in components (e.g. microcomputers in washing machines and televisions) to enhance product performance, manufacturing process productivity, or savings in maintenance and repair.

Innovation is potentially a strategic option for all organisations. Organisational innovation, and innovation based on the acquisition of new technology, are possible strategies in the service sector, the public sector and not-for-profit organisations. In most developed economies information and communication technologies (ICTs) are penetrating virtually all economic sectors with their potential to form the basis for innovation. Incorporating this new technology within organisations itself requires a capacity for change.

'Innovation' is frequently used interchangeably with 'change', or 'invention'. However, in the management context, Schumpeter's clear distinction between invention and innovation must be emphasised, as summarised here by Christopher Freeman:

> An *invention* is an idea, a sketch or model for a new or improved device, product, process or system. Such inventions may often (not always) be patented but they do not necessarily lead to technical *innovations*. In fact the majority do not. An *innovation* in the economic sense is accomplished only with the first *commercial* transaction involving the new product, process, system or device.
>
> (1982, p. 7).

Few inventions survive this translation into innovations. This *innovation process* that takes an invention and turns it into a marketable product or robust manufacturing, service or administrative process is both costly and lengthy. The time-gap between invention and innovation varies greatly between industries and sectors, and the process often generates new basic problems that require the development team to return again to the research laboratories.

You will remember the Zantac example from Book 1, where lead-times were so crucial. Another example is virtual reality (VR) which was first demonstrated at MIT in 1968 (Negroponte, 1995). After considerable investment by the US Department of Defense, VR was first used in embryonic form in the 1970s to train pilots and for other military purposes. VR was then taken up by the entertainment industry. VR finally arrived as Personal Computer (PC) add-on and in arcade games in 1995 – a gestation period from invention to affordable commercial product (innovation) of some 27 years. This was because VR required the complementary innovation of inexpensive, powerful PCs in order to be an affordable entertainment product.

These examples point to some of the central questions about the strategic management of innovation that emerge in the literature, which have importance to you both as MBA students and as managers:

- What determines the rate and direction of innovation and technical progress?
- Does technological innovation result more from technological developments or from market-pull?
- How can organisations grow and sustain the strategic capabilities necessary for innovation on an ongoing basis?
- What are the roles of customers and users in the innovation process?
- Are creativity and management fundamentally incompatible?
- How do you balance the need to support and encourage creativity and change, while providing stability and continuity?
- What organisational structures and cultural forms best provide support for innovative activity as a dynamic capability?
- How can cost and risk be minimised, and lead-times reduced?

1.2 LEARNING OBJECTIVES OF THIS BOOK

After studying this book, you should be able to:
- demonstrate how and why innovation may be both a source of advantage and an external threat, and relate this to the sources of competitive advantage discussed in previous books
- identify different types of product and process innovation
- identify generic aspects of innovation that are transferable across different organisational contexts

- evaluate current conceptual approaches to the management of the innovation process
- identify principal ways in which organisations acquire and manage the capabilities and resources that enable them to innovate, and relate this understanding to your own organisation
- demonstrate how innovation is a function of (formal and informal) organisational processes
- apply an understanding of the inter-organisational context of innovation to discussions on strategy in your own organisation.

1.3 SHAPE, SCOPE AND CONTENT OF THIS BOOK

Thinking about innovation requires us to think strategically about both the external environment and internal organisational processes, and about links between the two. This book connects the analysis of industry, sector, and the external environment to the strategic management of individual innovations within organisations.

The complex organisational and inter-organisational processes that result in innovative products, processes and systems will be explored. As in previous books we emphasise the centrality of organisational capabilities, and the utilisation and orchestration of resources. The strategic management of innovation requires cutting across many boundaries both within organisations, such as that between business strategy and corporate strategy and between organisations, since innovation is the result of inter-organisational knowledge, technology and people transfers.

Section 2 looks at the macro-economic dimensions of innovation, seeing innovation as both a threat in the competitive environment, and as the source of strategic advantage for some organisations. In order to understand the dynamics of innovation, we look at the concepts of technological paradigms and trajectories, as well as developing a typology of innovations. We look at process innovation, innovation in service-sector and not-for-profit organisations, and explore the interdependencies between product and process innovation, as well as patterns of diffusion of innovations.

Section 3 explains the drivers, sources, enablers and inhibitors of innovation, and identifies the strategic factors that condition the success and failure of innovation in organisations. It examines how organisations create advantage through innovation. Then the factors and inputs that drive innovation and the key dichotomy between technology-push and market-pull are discussed. This section also briefly addresses the question of investment and risk in innovation. It closes with a framework for identifying the strategic innovation options open to organisations, and related key success factors.

Section 4 places our analysis of strategies for innovation in a variety of contexts and sectors, looking particularly at service-sector organisations, large firms, small firms and mature industries. Section 5 is concerned with the strategic challenge of building and sustaining the capability to innovate in organisations. We see innovation as an outcome of organisational processes that must be supported by appropriate structures and management practices. These include the process of knowledge management and collaboration as a source of resources for innovation.

2 Frameworks for understanding innovation

2.1 Innovation and macro-environmental change

Joseph Schumpeter, more than any economist of the twentieth century, challenged received economic wisdom in locating innovation at the centre of economic activity. His analysis placed great importance on the historically destabilising impacts of significant or radical innovations such as the printing press, the steam engine, electrical power, and the railways. You were introduced in Book 4 to Schumpeter's (1934) concept of 'creative destruction', which he used to describe this radical process.

For example, one hundred years ago road transportation in Europe based on the horse was still a major economic sector employing hundreds of thousands. Motorised road transport wiped out harness making, farriers, horse trading and other ancillary trades as viable economic activities, although it did, at the same time, create entirely new ones. For Schumpeter, economic progress did not result from small improvements. He saw innovations as 'historic and irreversible changes in the way of doing things. ... innovations are changes in production functions which cannot be decomposed into infinitesimal steps. Add as many mail coaches as you please, you will never get a railroad by so doing' (1935; p. 7).

Innovation, from this perspective, is a discontinuous phenomenon (a step change) which shifts technology and competition onto an entirely new path, stimulating economic change on a grand scale. Managers have always had to develop strategies to deal with innovations in their competitive environment which directly affect their ability to survive economically but whose significance at the time is hard to evaluate. For example, the Ford Model T automobile was introduced in 1908. If you were managing director of a US harness makers in 1910, would you continue to take on apprentices, and would you consider investing in new leather-working machinery in order to be competitive in your market-place?

Activity 2.1

One hundred years after the harness makers were being replaced by the fitters and motor mechanics, do you perceive any technologies today that may be in the same position of Schumpeterian 'discontinuity'? Which professions and trades do you perceive to be currently under threat from new technologies? What are the implications of these threats for the strategist?

Discussion

The cluster of technologies generally labelled 'information and communications technology' (ICT) have for two decades been identified as being capable of the kind of major discontinuities

The Ford Model T automobile, introduced in 1908, and the mass-production techniques used to build it, shifted technology and competition onto an entirely new path, stimulating economic change on a grand scale

described by Schumpeter. Predictions of mass unemployment amongst clerical and office workers have perhaps been disguised by the time-lags involved in adjusting working practices to take full advantage of ICTs – we tend to use ICT to provide electronic duplicates of filing cabinets rather than to abolish them (indeed, the need to make such adjustments has been one of the themes of 'business process re-engineering'). ICT has transformed office work, but has been slow to replace the many people whose job still involves moving paper documents around. The advent of speech-input computers (again, heralded for almost two decades) may have a similar effect on word-processing and filing tasks.

Recent years have seen the replacement of typesetters by desk-top publishing in the printing industry, draughtsmen by computer-aided design (CAD) systems, welders and paint sprayers by robots in the automotive sector, continuous process plant operatives and train drivers by automatic systems.

The application of ICTs across virtually all organisational functions, in virtually all economic sectors, has led to the transformation, rather than the obliteration, of many job categories. Employment opportunities have, to an extent, grown in the service sector and new industries, such as multimedia entertainment and information providers, computer games and Internet service providers. However, just as early automation replaced manual labour, it is highly likely that computer systems will increasingly substitute for information-

related tasks – such as dealing with telephone inquiries, order processing, bookings and reservations, information searches, and customer help-lines. In fifty years' time historians may view the current period as one of ICT-induced 'creative destruction'.

2.1.1 Long waves, paradigms and trajectories

The *creative* half of the *creative destruction* dyad was linked by Schumpeter both to major economic upswings in the world economy and to the activities of entrepreneurs. He argued that 'innovations do not remain isolated events, and are not evenly distributed in time ... on the contrary, they tend to cluster, to come about in bunches, simply because first some and then most firms follow in the wake of successful innovation' (1939, p. 75).

He attributed this phenomenon, now known as Schumpeterian *swarming* of innovations, to the profit-seeking actions of entrepreneurs. Other entrepreneurs, seeing exceptional profits being made by first entrants, jump on the bandwagon and invest in their own innovative activity. This is similar to the process described in Porter's 'five forces' model (Book 3) as an attractive industry with high growth potential attracts new entrants and potential substitutes in pursuit of superior profits. In his later writings, Schumpeter came to acknowledge the increasing domination of large firms and corporate R&D in innovation, but it is his emphasis on entrepreneurial innovation that underpinned his exploration of innovation and growth.

Entrepreneurial innovation and the swarming of imitators provided Schumpeter with a mechanism to explain the massive fluctuations in the capitalist economy – the 40-to-60 year cycles of economic depressions and booms that characterise the period from around 1750 to the present. Schumpeter termed these Kondratiev cycles, after the Russian economist Nikolai Kondratiev, who linked such cycles to changes in investment activity. Schumpeter explored the link between technological innovation and these *long waves*, and in so doing laid the groundwork for a theory of economic change based on technological innovation.

Though debate still rages about the existence of long waves and the direction of causality (does innovation stimulate economic growth, or is it the other way round?) there is much evidence to support Schumpeter's hypothesis that economic upswings coincide with a *swarming* of innovations and particularly the diffusion of clusters of innovations throughout the economy. This diffusion process involves further development and innovation as the technology is scaled-up, adapted, improved and modified to reach into new economic sectors and activities.

This pattern of major technological innovations followed by a period of smaller or incremental innovations has led to the idea of technological paradigms and trajectories. Dosi (1982) drew on Nelson and Winter's (1982) suggestion that there are 'natural trajectories' of technological progress. Paradigms set the agenda for future progress, until they are replaced by new ones. For example, radical technological innovations such as semiconductors provide the change that defines a new ICT paradigm. Once the major technological breakthrough has been made, technological progress reverts to incremental change along the trajectory defined by the new paradigm. Technological questions, problems and opportunities are implicit in the adopted paradigm. In this way, generations of ever-faster microprocessors and greater concentrations of circuits in memory chips emerge as technology progresses along the trajectory. In the pharmaceutical industry, the innovation of monoclonal antibodies has led to a whole new strain of drugs developing incrementally along the trajectory set by the first innovation.

Technology changes faster, and more radically, than social and institutional systems, and the ability of organisations to use it effectively. This has major implications for strategic management at the level of the organisation. The patterns of organisation and institutions (such as education and training systems) tailored to the old paradigm may be inappropriate when the paradigm shifts. The organisation of work in relation to technological paradigms is central to past transformations, as in the diffusion of Fordist mass-production methods. Today, for example, we can see that the Fordist paradigm's need for semi-skilled and unskilled labour has left a legacy across Europe of unemployed people who do not have the appropriate skills required for new knowledge-intensive organisations.

Activity 2.2

New paradigms require new sets of skills. What are the strategic implications of paradigmatic technological change for the management of the public education system in your country?

Discussion

The answer to this question will partly depend on the role of the public sector vis-à-vis training in your country. In many countries the policy through the 1980s and 1990s has been for the public sector to increasingly withdraw from training, leaving this to the private sector. These countries still have to cope with the implications of paradigmatic technological change for their educational system and syllabus, both at school and university levels. New technological paradigms with rapid innovation, in the ICT area or in pharmaceuticals, demand new sets of employees' skills that require a knowledge base which the education system may not be designed to provide. To pursue the metaphors used earlier, the education systems must stop educating large numbers of people to be suitable apprentice horse-harness makers, or manufacturers of mail-coaches. This is a strategic challenge for educationalists, since there are time-lags in developing new curricula, training new teachers, appointing new lecturers, or retraining existing personnel. Strategic management in education must therefore develop capabilities to track and keep pace with developments, in the same way that commercial organisations must do.

At the present time, for example, UK university courses in software engineering span a curriculum including Cobol programming (1950s technology), structured analysis and design (1970s–80s), formal methods (1980s), and object-orientation (1980s–90s). Formal methods represent a radical approach to software development based on mathematical proof (as an alternative paradigm to 'hacking'). Many graduates of these courses have a background in formal methods of software development that they do not use in their jobs, because formal methods have not yet been widely adopted by industry – in part, ironically, because of a lack of appropriately skilled software engineers (Quintas, 1994). Educationalists must therefore, like their commercial counterparts, make strategic choices under conditions of change and uncertainty, and adopt innovative approaches to curriculum development. Close links with the leading-edge organisations in any field helps here, since these may have to instigate their own education and training programmes in new fields, until the public system catches up.

The paradigmatic view of technological innovation should not be seen as supporting a technological determinism argument – that is, that technology is outside economic and social systems and is driving events in some autonomous way. Rather, Dosi (1982) emphasises that the selection of a new technological paradigm is an historical process which combines economic, institutional and political forces through, for example, decisions to invest in R&D or create subsidised markets for emergent technologies (such as government support for nuclear technology in France and the UK, military and space programme support for semiconductors in the USA). A paradigm therefore has an exclusion effect, as do all types of strategic decisions: alternative paths may be ignored and deprived of funding and resources for R&D (e.g. alternative sources of energy such as wave power). This is a path-dependency model, discussed in connection with building capabilities in Book 4. However, as in all strategic thinking, it is important to be wary of simplistic interpretations based on a *linear model* of technological history implicit in the idea of trajectories. Linear models are unhelpful in explaining complex phenomena.

The complexity of managing and sustaining innovation, and of coping with innovation occurring in the environment, requires tools and frameworks able to analyse incremental change whilst allowing for radical, paradigmatic changes which are most likely to emanate from elsewhere.

Organisations need to develop strategies that equip them with an evolving set of capabilities and resources that enable them to survive and prosper in conditions of technological and market uncertainty and change. That is why in Book 1 it was argued that strategies based on 'fit' are not enough; there is also a need for strategies based on 'stretch'.

Kodama (1995) sees a new techno-economic paradigm emerging:

> For years it has been said that innovation is achieved by breaking through the boundaries of existing technology. Recent innovations in mechatronics and opto-electronics, however, make it more appropriate to view innovation as the *fusion* of different types of technology rather than as a series of technical breakthroughs. Fusion means more than a combination of different technologies; it invokes an arithmetic in which one plus one makes three.
>
> (1995, p. 9)

This new paradigm is therefore about the strategic *integration* of technologies, requiring managerial skills that can span disciplines and facilitate communication between different specialists. Kodama's view is based, however, on recent Japanese experience of perceived paradigm changes. In later sections of this book we will explore alternative accounts of the current and emerging patterns of innovation, and identify their implications for strategic thinking.

2.1.2 Incremental and radical innovation

Whilst our definition of innovation emphasises the first commercial launch or use of the new product, process or system as the defining event, it is clear that innovations do not emerge into the world as fully developed technologies or processes. Innovations that start as radical breakthroughs require a subsequent period of incremental development to fully exploit their technical and organisational possibilities.

Not all innovations are of the radical or 'blockbuster' type. The vast majority are incremental innovations – gradual improvements in products, processes or systems, each building on the former and following a developmental pathway that is coherent and cumulative. Counter to Schumpeter's view, such incremental innovation has been shown, over time, to be capable of even greater technical progress and productivity increases than major one-off innovations. Banbury and Mitchell (1995) concluded that incremental product innovation is crucially important to the business survival and performance of firms already active in a product-market.

Schumpeter's ideas have been criticised on several counts. In addition to his downplaying of the importance of incremental innovation, 'creative destruction' fails to take account of the fact that old technologies, products and processes may co-exist alongside the latest innovations for many years (filing cabinets and typewriters co-exist with computers, black and white televisions with colour TVs, etc.). In some cases the arrival of the newcomer stimulates a period of renewed innovation in the old technology. This is known as the 'steamship phenomenon', so called because the arrival of steam vessels in the nineteenth century triggered a flurry of innovation in sailing ship technology as these vessels strove to compete. A similar response can be seen today in photography, as traditional cameras based on chemical reaction in light-sensitive film compete with fully opto-electronic devices.

2.2 AN INNOVATION TYPOLOGY

The importance of both incremental and radical innovation for strategy is now widely accepted. However, we clearly need a more rigorous framework within which to discuss degrees of innovation and diffusion. Are we, for example, talking about *industries* (such as electricity generation) or individual technologies (such as semiconductors)? We require a framework that seeks to locate individual product and process innovations within industrial or sectoral contexts.

The distinction between *incremental* and *radical* innovation should be fairly clear to you by now. Incremental innovation happens cumulatively and continuously in most sectors. The key point is that radical innovations could not occur by incremental developments of existing products, processes or systems. Continuous developments of coal-fired power stations did not lead to nuclear power stations; and incremental refinement of mass production manufacturing, with ever shorter task-cycle times, would not lead to team-based manufacture requiring multi-skilled workers. However, it is also clear that incremental innovation can, over time, lead to significant advances and competitive advantages for organisations, as learning-by-doing and capability-building lead to cumulatively significant changes in product or process performance.

The strategic management of innovation must also take account of the fact that innovations may be interdependent and have a systemic quality. The adoption of any innovation may depend on *complementary innovations* occurring in the market-place, as with the example of virtual reality computer games and simulations requiring powerful PCs. Freeman (1982) suggests the term *new technological systems* to describe constellations of innovations that are technologically and economically interlinked. Technological interdependence is evident, for example, between petrochemicals, synthetic materials and plastics, and the innovations in process machinery required to produce them. Organisational and institutional innovation are also vital components of new technological systems. For example, the availability of consumer credit is an essential component of the creation of markets for new consumer products such as cars or televisions, as is the presence of appropriate skills in the workforce to enable the adoption of product and process innovations.

We now have three categories – incremental innovation, radical innovation, and new technological systems, which include complementary innovations. Can this analysis account for all types of innovation, from organisation-level product and process improvement through to economy-wide transformations? Freeman suggests that a fourth category is needed. He calls this a change of *techno-economic paradigm*, a cluster of innovations and new technological systems, as well as associated organisational and institutional changes. The key characteristic of innovations in the techno-economic paradigm is that they pervade the whole economy. They must therefore meet the following criteria:

- clearly perceived low and rapidly falling costs
- apparently unlimited supply over a long period
- potential for use and application throughout the economic system, both directly and indirectly, in products and processes.

These criteria were met by the techno-economic paradigm surrounding oil and petrochemicals which underpinned the post-war economic boom, and, according to Freeman, are met today by the ICT techno-economic paradigm.

This results in a *typology of innovations*:

- incremental
- radical
- new technological system (including complementary innovations)
- techno-economic paradigm.

Activity 2.3

Which of these four types of innovation are of concern to you as a manager making *strategic* decisions?

Discussion

They should all be, but the decisions in each category have different time horizons. Strategic management is concerned with creating the capabilities that enable the organisation to innovate. This means exploiting the core capabilities and expertise of the organisation in order to make incremental changes in processes, products and services. In some cases your organisation may itself be pursuing radical innovations; but if this is not the case, you need to be aware of external developments that may have radical implications for your activities. The implications of systemic and complementary innovation are vitally important – in order to see your own activities in relation to external complementary developments, which include innovations that, as we saw in Book 4, may be available as complementary assets. Finally, a change of techno-economic paradigm is a phenomenon that is hard to detect, let alone make strategic decisions about, while it is happening. Nevertheless, with the benefit of hindsight we can unquestionably detect major upheavals in technological, institutional, economic and social systems. The challenge for strategists is to develop a real-time awareness of major changes and take the implications of these into account in our strategic thinking.

In addition to the scale and scope of innovation, we have also emphasised the important distinction between *product* and *process* innovation. Since it is an option open to all types of organisations, we now explore the concept of *process innovation* in greater depth.

2.3 PROCESS INNOVATION

As well as launching innovative products, organisations can innovate in the processes that they carry out in order to achieve their objectives. Process innovation might focus on the introduction of new working practices or quality management regimes, and is likely to include the introduction of new technology, particularly information technology. The latter may require new skills and the adoption of new working practices in order to improve process productivity or output quality. Davenport (1993) gives some recent examples of process innovations in both manufacturing and service sector organisations:

> IBM Credit reduced the time to prepare a quote for buying or leasing a computer from seven days to one, while increasing the number of quotes prepared tenfold. Moreover, more than half its quotes are now issued by computer. Federal Mogul, a billion-dollar auto parts manufacturer, reduced the time to develop a new part prototype from twenty weeks to twenty days, thereby tripling the likelihood of customer acceptance. Mutual Benefit Life, a large insurance company seeking to offset a declining real estate portfolio, halved the cost associated with its policy underwriting and issuance process. Even the US Internal Revenue Service achieved successful process innovation, collecting 33% more dollars from delinquent taxpayers with half its former staff and a third fewer branch offices.
>
> *(1993, p. 2)*

'Business process re-engineering' has been one approach to process innovation. However, as Davenport makes clear:

> Re-engineering is only part of what is necessary in the radical change of processes; it refers specifically to the design of the new process. The term process innovation encompasses the envisioning of new work strategies, the actual process design activity, and the implementation of change in all its complex technological, human, and organisational dimensions.
>
> *(1993, p. 2)*

According to Rothwell (1992), process innovation is likely to involve non-technical innovations of four kinds:

- organisational innovation, e.g. the modern logistical outsourcing arrangements by large retailers, using centralised automated warehousing technology

- management innovation, e.g. project teams instead of departments
- production innovations, e.g. a quality control circle
- commercial/marketing innovations, e.g. direct selling or leasing.

Innovations that have systemic qualities, requiring changes across many functional areas of the organisation, or innovations that require combinations of skills and expertise that cut across disciplines and functions – Kodama's 'fusions' – are likely to have major organisational implications for the adopting organisation. Remember the Novotel mini-case from Book 4 which described exactly such a combination of cross-functional adaptations, arising from systemic innovation.

Much process innovation occurs when no technology is involved at all. Often technology is assumed to be the key variable in process innovations that are in fact essentially organisational. For example, the just-in-time (JIT) or *kanban* system is a way of organising the assembly of manufactured products so that the component parts arrive at the assembly-line 'just-in-time'. This removes the need for large inventory stocks which are expensive and take up large amounts of production space. JIT was introduced in Japan in the 1950s by Toyota, and although it is dependent on crucial and precise flows of information, it was for many years achieved without computer systems. *Kanban* literally translates as 'visible record' – a ticket was physically delivered from the assembly workers to suppliers to advise of the requirement for components. Of course, communications between assembly workers and component suppliers are now invariably handled via computer systems, but the technology is secondary to the organisational innovation of JIT production.

Indeed, Rosabeth Moss Kanter seeks to counter the prevailing focus on technology with an analysis of innovation based on people, and social and organisational processes:

> The term 'innovation' makes people think first about technology: new products and new methods for making them. ... If most people were asked to list some of the major innovations of the last few years, microprocessors and computer-related devices would be mentioned frequently. Fewer people would mention new tax laws or the creation of enterprise zones, even though those are innovations too. Fewer still, if any, would be likely to mention such innovations as quality circles or problem-solving task forces. This is unfortunate, for our emerging world requires more social and organisational innovation. Indeed, it is by now a virtual truism that if technical innovation runs far ahead of complementary social and organisational innovation, its use in practice can be either dysfunctional or negligible. The advanced technology incorporated in nuclear plants clearly needs more organisational innovation to prevent the frequent breakdowns of both components and human controls. Even many 'productivity improvements' rest, at root, on innovations that determine how jobs are designed or how departments are composed.
>
> Innovation refers to the processes of bringing in any new, problem-solving idea into use. Ideas for re-organising, cutting costs, putting in new budget systems, improving communication, or assembling products in teams are also innovations. Innovation is the generation, acceptance, and implementation of new ideas, processes, products, or services.
>
> *(1984, p. 20)*

Reflection

Consider your own organisation, or one with which you are familiar, and identify examples of process innovations that (i) depend on the introduction of new technology; (ii) do not depend on the introduction of new technology; and (iii) are examples of the introduction of new technology that has resulted in, or requires, complementary organisational or non-technical innovation. Which of these have had the greatest strategic impact on the working practices in your organisation, or on productivity or product quality?

2.4 PRODUCT AND PROCESS INTERDEPENDENCE

The distinction between product and process innovation is a useful one, but we need to be aware that the two types of innovation may have a dynamic interdependence over time. Strategic advantage may be gained by exploiting this interdependence. For example, the major banks developed electronic funds transfer (EFT) as a process innovation to speed up the transfer of money between branches, and then between banks. The productivity benefits and cost savings that resulted from the reduction of paper transfers were significant. The first phase, focused on automation of back-office tasks (basic data processing) enabled the UK banking sector to improve productivity to a 4.5 per cent annual growth rate by the early 1970s, when the volume of banking transactions was growing by 8 per cent per year. As the demand for banking services slowed from the mid-1970s, the banks continued to invest in ICTs at an increased rate over the period 1975–81. In a period of enhanced competition, innovative banks turned their ICT investment to improving the quality of services. The EFT systems were process innovations that also provided the infrastructure upon which new products could be based. In particular, they enabled the banks to introduce ATMs (automatic teller machines) that provided customers with 24-hour cash withdrawals, balance checks, and other services via the 'through-the-wall' computer terminals at their branches. This is also an example of a classic economy of scope, to which you were introduced in Book 4.

Activity 2.4

Consider whether this mix of process and product innovation (as in the banking example) applies also to public-sector and not-for-profit organisations? Are there parallels in the innovative use of information and communications technologies (ICTs) by organisations in these sectors?

Discussion

There are similar patterns across the public services and not-for-profit sectors. Barras (1986, 1990) has developed a model of innovation which is generalisable across all types of service sector organisations, including not-for-profits. The Barras model suggests that the pattern of innovation in service sector and not-for-profit organisations is a reverse product cycle, *since the progression is from process innovation to product innovation, the reverse of the conventional product cycle based on manufacturing industry.*

Table 2.1 shows this pattern of innovation in UK local government, with the insurance and accountancy service sectors included for comparison.

Table 2.1 ICT-based innovation in service sectors

Type of innovation	1 Improved efficiency	2 Improved quality	3 New services
Period	1970s	1980s	1990s
Computer technology	Centralised mainframes	On-line systems; minis and micros	Networks; PCs
Service sector applications			
Local government	Corporate financial systems (e.g. payroll) and computerised records	Departmental service delivery e.g. housing allocation, databases of roads and land usage, social services registers of at-risk children	Public information services (e.g. Viewdata, library information services); self-help and self-service systems for citizens
Insurance	Computerised policy records	On-line policy quotations	Complete on-line service
Accountancy	Computer audit; internal time recording	Computerised management accounting	Fully automated audit and accounts

(Source: developed from Barras, 1986, p. 166)

2.5 DIFFUSION OF INNOVATIONS

The process by which innovations are taken up by increasing numbers of organisations and spread through the economy is known as *diffusion*. Two factors affecting the diffusion of innovation are particularly relevant to managers. These are *network externalities* and *standardisation*.

Network externalities are factors that are external to the innovation itself, but which condition the pace and scope of diffusion. Network externalities are most easily illustrated by the example of telecommunications networks. Your organisation is unlikely to be willing to join a telecom network which was only connected to 100 other subscribers: the value to a new subscriber of joining a network is conditional on the number of other individuals or organisations connected to the network. The network externalities principle affects the diffusion patterns of many different kinds of innovations. For example, the usefulness of cars is dependent on there being service stations where fuel can be obtained, and there will only be a wide network of service stations if there is a critical mass of car users. The lack of such a critical mass inhibits the take-up of the innovation by more users. Organisations may therefore have to invest forward or backward in different parts of their industry supply chain to encourage take-up of their innovation. A well-known example of this was the food manufacturing company Birds Eye in the 1950s providing grocery retailers with freezers to encourage them to stock the new frozen food products. The frozen foods could not be stored or sold without such additional supporting technology, which was first paid for by the investor company on behalf of its potential customers.

The second factor is standardisation. When new innovations are first introduced, potential adopters may be inhibited from taking them up because there is uncertainty as to whether this particular solution will be widely adopted. Eventually a 'dominant design' may emerge which sets the standard for the industry. A well-known example is the VCR standard VHS (developed by JVC Matsushita) which won the "standards" battle with Sony's and Philips' rival technologies. The presence of a standard or dominant design reduces the risk of adopting an innovation, and so diffusion accelerates. Fighting to establish its innovation as the industry standard is now a critical strategic weapon used by innovating companies to gain and retain market share and returns on these expensive long-term investments.

We will now look at the processes within organisations which determine their ability to innovate for strategic advantage.

3 Innovation and strategy

As we stated in the introduction to this book, strategy is concerned with creating the capability to innovate, and with appropriating profits and sustaining advantage from innovation. However, there are no simple formulas that can deliver these objectives. Quinn (1986) described the strategic management of innovation in large corporations as 'managed chaos'. He suggested that the unpredictable nature of innovation precludes a reliance on formal, planned processes – innovation is non-linear, with large elements of chance. If formal planning strategies were appropriate more companies could emulate the successful ones, innovation would be more common, and advantage from innovation would be less. Studies of innovation emphasise again and again the non-linearity and multi-factor nature of the innovation process. If we look, retrospectively, for the sources and inputs to any particular innovation it is often not possible to identify the starting point (Langrish *et al.*, 1972). This means that rational formal planning processes are rarely possible in the context of developing and marketing an individual innovation.

Let us revisit our quotation from Sony's former Chairman:

> The innovation process begins with a mandate which must be set at the highest levels of the corporation by identifying goals and priorities and once identified, these must be communicated all the way down the line.

This statement suggests that senior management provide the mandate, set goals and priorities, and establish structures and processes to communicate them throughout the organisation. Does this mean that senior managers identify technologies or organisational innovations as goals and priorities, or do they circumscribe broader frameworks within which others make choices and pursue particular innovations? Incremental innovation, too, may be a source of strategic advantage in the longer term, since its effects may be cumulatively significant. Even incremental innovation must therefore be considered to have implications for strategy, but can it be *managed strategically*?

It *is* possible for organisations of all types to develop a strategy for innovation which copes with unpredictability and complexity in a dynamic way. This begins with seeing any individual innovation as a result of *dynamic processes* that require the development and sustainability of organisational capabilities. As well as setting agendas and objectives, and providing a mandate to underpin and encourage innovative activity throughout the organisation, senior management must also ensure that skills, expertise and other resources are present, and that the organisational structures and culture support innovation in a dynamic way. This means that strategies to promote innovation need to continuously ensure that the organisation is capable of linking the potentials provided by technological and organisational change with market opportunities.

One obviously strategic area is the investment in the organisation's intellectual capital, and particularly its human resources, education and training. In many sectors innovation is only possible if organisations commit significant resources to formal R&D activity. Placing the R&D director on the board and ring-fencing a proportion of investment capital for longer-term R&D is essential in high-technology industries. The flows of information within the organisation, and between it and the suppliers of new knowledge and technology, take on increasing strategic importance as technologies and product-markets become more complex and global. Increasingly, organisations also have to make links across their organisational boundaries in order to innovate. Organisational processes and systems which not only create and access new knowledge, but also protect the knowledge base of the organisation, are vital.

All these issues require managers to think strategically about innovation. In many sectors the nature of technical change and competition means that not to innovate is to die. However, it is not always necessary, or even advantageous, to be an 'offensive' innovator – the company first to the market with a wholly new type of product (as exemplified by the De Havilland company with the Comet jet airliner, or Sony in VCRs). Most organisations can scarcely avoid being 'defensive' or 'imitative' innovators.

3.1 CREATING ADVANTAGE THROUGH INNOVATION

Read Chapter 11 in the Set Book and complete Activity 3.1.

Activity 3.1

As you read the chapter, consider the following questions:

1. Noting the examples of innovations used in Chapter 11 of the Set Book, would you say this account provides a comprehensive coverage of innovation? What is missing or downplayed?
2. Note the pattern of technology development and dissemination suggested in Set Book Figure 11.1. What, in your view, does the Set Book consider to be the driver of technological innovation?
3. Recalling previous books, what are the implications of network effects, technological uncertainty and the importance of complementary resources for the strategic management of innovation in any organisation?
4. Is 'innovation' synonymous with 'R&D'? Which parts or functional areas of the organisation should or should not be concerned with innovation?

Discussion

1 Chapter 11 mostly concentrates on product innovations, largely ignoring process innovation. The examples tend to be the more notable innovations towards the 'radical' end of the product innovation spectrum, with little reference to incremental innovations – which are far more numerous.

2 Figure 11.1 suggests that innovation is driven by advances in knowledge and invention. The 'demand side' (i.e. the market) is portrayed as a recipient of the innovation, but has no input to the innovation process. This is essentially a 'technology-push' model. We will discuss alternatives to this model in Section 3.2 of this book.

3 This a big question. You will recall in Book 4, when we discussed the notion of organisations having resources and capabilities, the latter included the capability to access and utilise resources from outside the organisation. The common theme that unites the implications of network effects, technological uncertainty and the importance of complementary resources for innovation, is that organisations do not develop innovations in a vacuum. They must be able to access technology and knowledge from external sources, share risks, ensure the presence of resources they do not own (e.g. an electricity supply network for electric car makers), and consider how they might help other complementary suppliers develop the network externalities that would make their own products and services more attractive. Innovation, then, is in many ways an inter-organisational process. We will return to these issues in later sections of this book.

4 *Innovation is a broader concept than that circumscribed by the notion of R&D. The R&D department is clearly a major locus of innovative activity in large organisations (small organisations do not tend to have R&D departments). However, remember that innovation assumes that the product, process or service has reached the market, or is commercially useful. For manufactured products, therefore, the production engineering and manufacturing departments would have been involved well before the product reaches the market. We should also assume that finance, marketing, sales and maintenance departments will have been involved in product design, since they will have to sell and maintain it at a profit. So too, personnel and staff development will have been involved, particularly if recruitment or training is required. The answer, therefore, is that all functional areas of the organisation may be involved in innovation, although the input of some might be indirect.*

3.2 THE DRIVERS OF INNOVATION

In order to think about building the capabilities to innovate, we need to better understand the inputs to the innovation process. What *drives* innovation? Much of our understanding of this question comes from studies of *technological* innovation which have generated a debate between the notion that technological innovation has its own dynamic ('technology-push') and the idea that innovation results from demand ('market-pull').

In Book 3, Porter's 'industry analysis' approach viewed innovation as a threat from the external competitive environment, or as a strategy for changing the basis of competition, rather than innovation as the result of organisational processes. Mainstream neo-classical schools in economics also treat innovation as 'exogenous' (outside the economic system) like the discovery of new land masses or seams of gold. The alternative view is that innovation results from 'endogenous' (internal) processes within the economic system. It is self-evident that technological innovation is the result of human actions that take place within social, economic, institutional and organisational contexts. Countering the simplistic view that technology drives social change, Lewis Mumford argued over 60 years ago that:

> Technics and civilisation as a whole are the result of human choices and aptitudes and strivings ...the world of techniques is not isolated and self-contained.
>
> (1934, p. 6)

This view accords with a central theme in this course – that organisations make significant choices and build capabilities to execute strategies. Innovation results from such capabilities. This theme suggests strongly that, for any given organisation, innovation should be regarded as an emergent property of organisational processes – units must grow the ability to innovate. However, we have also seen in Section 2 that technology may also have its own dynamic, in the sense that once a new paradigm is selected, innovation occurs incrementally, broadly following the agenda laid down by the technological trajectory. In this sense, innovation is path-dependent as each new incremental innovation builds on the former ones. This progression depends crucially on the accumulation of knowledge and capabilities within organisations.

3.2.1 Science as a driver of innovation

The drivers of innovation change over time, with the maturing of both technology and industry. Kline (1989) suggests different types of drivers according to changing competition, the emergence of dominant designs, and the dominance of larger organisations when maturity is reached.

How far is science a driver of technological innovation? Table 3.1 suggests that nascent industries depend, in part, on inputs from science. Whilst the public perception of technology remains largely that technology is *applied science*, in reality, as already explained in Section 1.1, technology is not simply applied science, it is a body of knowledge concerning techniques, methods, and designs that work (Rosenberg, 1982; p. 143). This point – that technology is about techniques, methods and activities which include experiential knowledge – is important for our later discussions on the sources of knowledge that contribute to innovation, especially to the strategic challenges of *knowledge management* for innovation in Section 5.

Table 3.1 Drivers of innovation

Stage of industry	Common driver(s) of product innovations
Nascent	Radical invention
	Enabling science
Infant	Product designs
	Creating production processes
	Developing a market
Maturing	Stabilising designs
	Improvement in quality
	Reduction in costs
Obsolescent	Finding new markets
	Retraining workers

(Kline, 1989, p. 133)

Is scientific research a strategic concern for commercial organisations? Its importance depends on many factors, including the industrial sector, the maturity of the technology, the availability of scientific knowledge from external sources, and the levels of knowledge within the organisation. Of course, *science* covers a broad spectrum of activities from the pursuit of knowledge in *basic research*, through to *applied research* which seeks to solve particular problems that may be commercially defined. In most areas of science, commercial organisations cannot make the necessary investments in order to sustain the pursuit of basic research, and this therefore relies heavily on public funds.

Activity 3.2

If science is strategically important as an input to innovation, why should commercial organisations rely on public funding of basic research?

Discussion

This is primarily because:

- *there is very high uncertainty and risk in scientific research*
- *the difficulty of choosing, in advance, which scientific lines of inquiry will prove to be commercially rewarding*
- *the difficulty organisations have in appropriating the benefits from scientific research, which has long been considered a public good*
- *the existence of a time-lag between scientific discovery and commercial returns on investment.*

Advances in science and science-based innovations do, however, over time, undoubtedly have profound effects on the economy and competitive environment. From the end of the nineteenth century large corporations, recognising the commercial returns from science-based innovations, began establishing scientific research laboratories, some of which, like the Bell Laboratories in the USA, have won world renown. In recent years the gap between science and technology has, in many fields, begun to close significantly. Indeed, participation in some areas of commercial activity is only possible today with a strategic commitment to scientific research.

Biotechnology, which we discussed in the Biogen case in the Book 2 Reader article, is a prime example. Figure 3.1 shows the three generations of biotechnology, from basic brewing, fermentation and plant and animal breeding, through microbiological technology, to genetic engineering. The figure illustrates clearly the inputs from craft knowledge and technology, as well as science. However, it is apparent that participation in the third generation requires a commitment to R&D. Biotechnology experienced a Schumpeterian 'swarming' in the 1970s and 1980s, with many new start-up companies and spin-off companies from government-funded research institutions and universities in the USA. Note, therefore, that the basic, long-term research was publicly-funded.

In this period of swarming, the risk-taking entrepreneurs forming new-start companies were supported by very large sums of money invested into scientific research in US universities. Many university scientists acted similarly, attracting venture capital that was equally anxious to join the race for high growth and high profits. Sharp (1991) observes that the large pharmaceutical companies who had strong historic research links with chemistry and pharmacy departments were at a disadvantage to the start-ups, because biotechnology was emerging from the biological sciences. This is also, therefore, an example of a paradigm shift, and

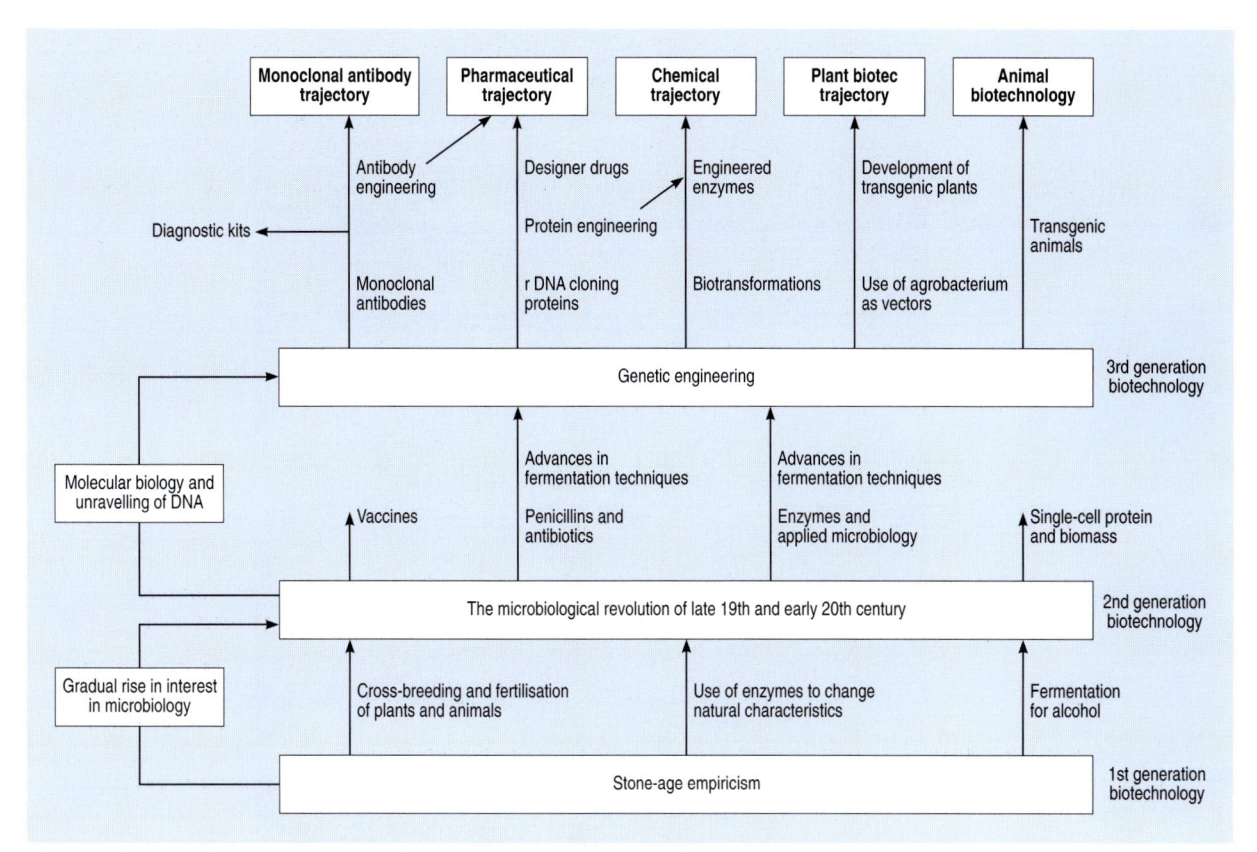

Figure 3.1 The three generations of biotechnology and the main areas of development of the new biotechnology (Sharp, 1991: p. 220)

therefore of high uncertainty, for the pharmaceutical industry. The industry had built capabilities and resources within its existing disciplines, which were now being outflanked by developments from an entirely different area of research. The small start-up firms were 'able to mobilise the cross-disciplinary teams – the geneticists, micro-biologists, protein chemists and biochemical engineers – necessary to take a project from workbench to pilot plant production; and they were able to try out ideas and take risks at which the larger firms would balk' (Sharp, 1991, p. 222).

However, as biotechnology start-up companies have matured, many of the more innovative and successful firms have been acquired by large firms (Genentech by Hoffman LaRoche in 1990; Biogen Europe by Glaxo in 1987). In many university research departments, the patent lawyers have moved in to ensure their sponsors' investments in the research are protected from the free flow of knowledge formerly associated with scientific discoveries in university departments. However, even in biotechnology, where the links with science are very close, other forms of technological knowledge must be applied in order to develop innovations. As Figure 3.1 shows, a range of complementary skills, resources and expertise must be present.

Although Biotechnology is undoubtedly a 'science-based' industry, the relationship between the scientific research and demand signals from the market place is complex. There are, it would seem, generic market needs for new strains of rice, wheat and other plants, for superior breeds of farm animals, or for new drugs and medical materials, such as blood. To some extent, biotechnology is a technology looking for applications, although the commercial interest and large-scale investment that has taken place suggests that there are many who believe that potential markets exist. Similarly, DuPont developed nylon in the 1930s through a

Wallace Carothers, the inventor of nylon. DuPont announced the world's first artificial fibre at the New York World's Fair on 27 October 1938. Nylon stockings first went on sale in upmarket department stores across the USA on 15 May 1940. Despite premium prices of $1.15 to $1.35, nearly five million pairs were sold on the first day alone. Apart from its huge commercial success, 'the invention of nylon marked the beginning of the modern era of the scientific design of materials' (quotation from *Enough for one Lifetime* by Matthew E. Hermes).

'mission-oriented' research programme searching for a polymer with the characteristics of silk. The market for such a fibre, if it could be developed, was relatively certain, given the price and popularity of silk. This future (or latent) demand for something that at present is not available is often the spur to R&D in new technologies.

3.3 TECHNOLOGY-PUSH OR MARKET-PULL?

The dominant strategic view of how innovation occurs has changed over time. Figure 3.2 shows three models of the innovation process, representing three generations of the dominant perceptions about the strategic management of innovation.

The traditional *linear model* of innovation shows science and technology 'pushing' the process. Most studies of innovation have suggested that this model is grossly over-simplified, not least because of the time-lag

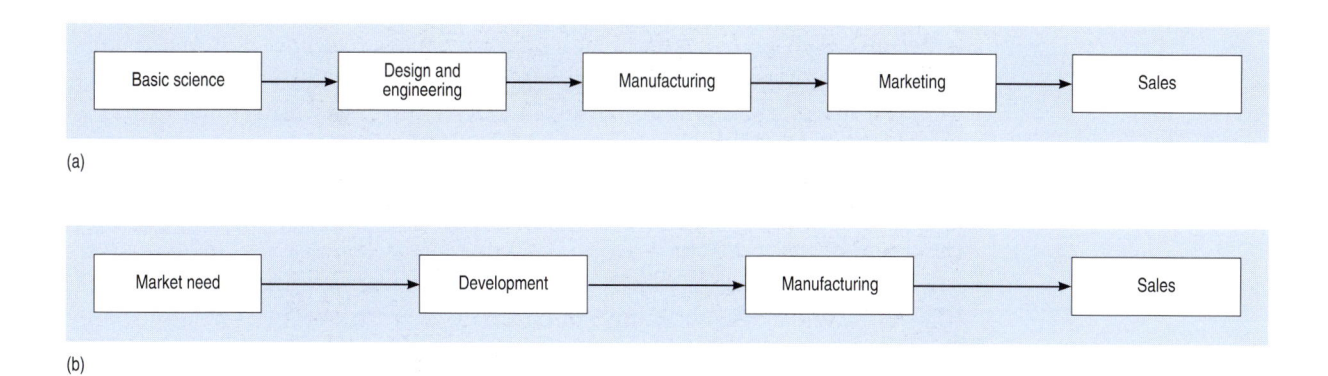

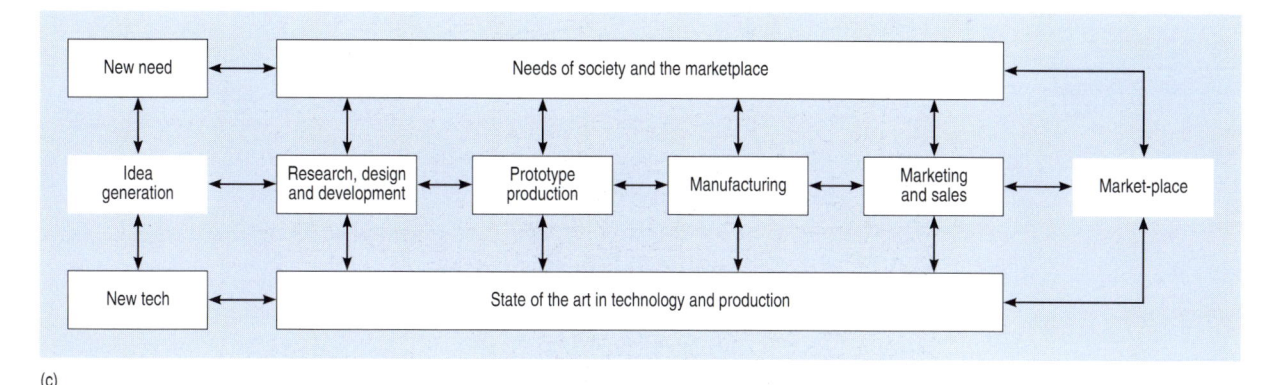

Figure 3.2 Three models of the innovation process: (a) technology-push (first generation) 1950s to mid-1960s; (b) market-pull (second generation) late 1960s to early 1970s; (c) 'coupling' model (third generation) mid-1970s to early 1980s (Rothwell, in Dodgson and Rothwell, 1994)

between scientific discoveries and the appearance of innovations which utilise them. Does the market really have no input over what may be a ten to twenty-five year period? However, until very recently, this form of linear model was dominant in shaping government policy towards innovation in many countries. It led to the assumption, for example, that government could fund research and development that it insisted was distanced from the market place, in the belief that firms would later translate the results from that R&D into commercially successful innovations. Such a policy proved flawed, because it misunderstood the strategic management of innovation at the firm level (Quintas and Guy, 1995).

The second graphic in Figure 3.2 depicts another linear model, this time with the market driving the innovation process forwards. Market signals provide the goal to be aimed at. One problem with this model is that the market does not usually demand innovations that have yet to appear, or for which there are no current reference technologies. There may be generic 'needs' or 'wants', such as for low-cost or long-shelf-life food, or more specific needs, such as a cure for Alzheimer's disease, or for a low-cost artificial fibre with the characteristics of silk. In the latter case the synthetic material is relatively easy to conceive in advance, since it is required to perform like an existing material. More radical technologies are less likely to result from specific market *demands*. Indeed this was the reason given by Sony for lack of market research on its Walkman: that no demand *could* have yet existed for such a product.

The context where the inputs of the market to innovation are most apparent is in supplier-customer relationships. Large primary contractors often pass know-how, technology and knowledge to smaller subcontractors and suppliers; thus the large-firm customer is a source of inputs to the innovation processes in the smaller organisation. This type of quasi-integration was discussed in Book 4 and may contribute to the effectiveness of either cost-leadership or differentiation strategies, for example by contributing to cost-reduction or quality-enhancement processes. Similarly, for the development of ICT-based innovations, the presence of 'sophisticated users' is often critical. Indeed, it is given as one key reason why the US has been successful in innovating and diffusing ICTs throughout the economy, in comparison with countries where there is a lower level of user capability. Sophisticated customers give high-quality feedback to suppliers and provide them with continual challenges that require innovative solutions (Hippel, 1976).

However, there are also dangers which may result from companies paying too much attention to the *immediate* needs and requirements of their current customers and thereby failing to innovate for future market needs. Organisations must develop strategies to manage this paradox: to balance their attention to their customers' immediate needs, while ensuring their future markets by building the dynamic capability to innovate in order to meet future demands.

The market may also drive firms to innovate in times of enhanced competition in mature industries. In the oil and gas industry, the effective end of the OPEC cartel's oligopoly and price collapse in 1986 ended a period in which the industry was essentially an attractive one, although vulnerable to political as well as market constraints. The investors in North Sea and Gulf of Mexico off-shore oil fields found themselves in possession of costly assets without economic viability at current oil price levels. Ironically, what followed was a new phase of innovation in submarine technology, deep-water oil and gas platforms, 3-D seismography, horizontal drilling technology and information systems for prospecting management. These innovations resulted from a need to reduce the costs of exploration and extraction and, in particular, to recover the 'sunk' investment in fixed assets. This example illustrates that negative messages from the market can also be a stimulus to innovation.

The third model in Figure 3.2 takes both the dynamics of technology and the needs of the market into account. This *coupling* model provides a much richer context in which innovation might occur. Innovation can be seen to be a dynamic process which responds to both market needs and technological opportunities. The strategic challenge is to develop the organisational capability to unite the technological and market potentials. The model also contains feedback loops occurring at every juncture, so that, for example, lessons from manufacturing or marketing may provide new inputs to R&D. Innovation is thus recognised to be a dynamic process in which initial goals and strategies will be refined and changed as the development process continues.

3.3.1 The new innovation paradigm

The coupling model, however, still describes an essentially sequential and compartmentalised process. From the mid-1980s, a fourth model has emerged. Organisations began to see innovation as an integrated process, where events happen in parallel and functional boundaries begin to blur. Japanese electronics and automobile companies adopted what has become known as the *rugby team* approach (Imai *et al.*, 1985) in which the organisation moves forward together in order to achieve its innovation objectives. The two key aspects of this are thus *integration* across functional areas, and *parallelism*, with the various elements of the innovation process happening concurrently. Figure 3.3 shows this fourth generation innovation process as it is used in new product development in Nissan. Group meetings cut vertically across the functional areas, providing integration. Note that marketing is shown to precede R&D, which may or may not be appropriate for a company in the automotive sector. This element of the model will vary by sector. The relevance of this integrated and parallel approach to innovation in many, if not all, sectors, is emphasised in this quotation from Peter Drucker:

> In pharmaceuticals, in telecommunications, in paper making, the traditional sequence of research, development, manufacturing, and marketing is being replaced by synchrony: specialists from all these functions work together as a team, from the inception of research to a product's establishment in the market.

(1988, p. 152)

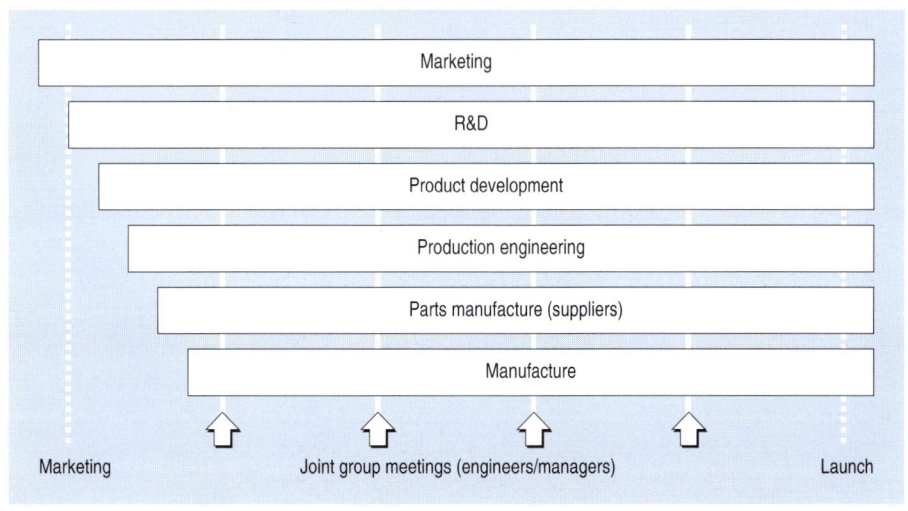

Figure 3.3 Integrated fourth-generation model of innovation (Graves, 1987)

No generalised model of the innovation process has yet been developed. However, eminent writers on innovation such as Kodama and Rothwell have suggested that innovation is moving into a new phase, based on elements such as knowledge creation, networking, technology fusion, customer focus and product customisation, and the application of ICTs to all aspects of the innovation process.

Rothwell (1994) identifies the sources of strategic advantage in this new 'fifth generation' innovation paradigm as the following:

- time-based strategy (faster, more efficient product development)
- development focus on quality and other non-price factors
- emphasis on corporate flexibility and responsiveness
- customer focus at the forefront of strategy
- strategic integration with primary suppliers
- strategies for horizontal technological collaboration
- electronic data processing strategies
- policy of total quality control.

Kodama's (1995) notion of the new techno-economic paradigm, introduced in Section 2, has many similar features but also emphasises the creation of knowledge through greater commitments to R&D,

technology fusion, inter-organisational collective learning, inter-industry competition, and the co-evolution of technology and institutions.

3.4 INVESTMENT IN INNOVATION

Few issues illustrate the strategic implications of investment decisions better than innovation. The challenges of investment in innovation are *uncertainty and risk* over the following dimensions:

- feasibility, including technological uncertainty
- cost of development
- appropriability
- time to market
- future demand
- future competitive environment
- return on investment.

The extent of uncertainty and risk is related to the maturity of the sector and the relative novelty of the innovation. Incremental innovation in relatively stable markets is obviously lower-risk than more radical innovations. However, the stability of markets can only ever be for limited periods – as the examples quoted previously of NCR, Goodyear tyres, and Xerox photocopiers illustrate. The future is uncertain, and new technologies and forms of competition may transform stable markets, negating organisations' investment in incremental innovation. The personal computer market has become used to incremental innovation, with power and memory size increasing at a predictable rate. Radical innovation may occur however, if, as Larry Ellison, the CEO of Oracle predicted in 1996, computing power becomes located remotely and accessed through a cable or telecommunications network.

The difficulty of prediction, and therefore the certainty of risk, is fundamental to investment in innovation. In some sectors this risk is endemic, for example in the pharmaceuticals industry, where only around one in twelve R&D projects results in a commercially successful innovation. Even then, appropriating the return on investment depends on the immutability of the innovation, as the Tagamet and Zantac example showed. The investment strategies of many organisations are often characterised as being *risk averse*, meaning that they seek to maximise certainty for investments made. Often this means taking a short-term view, since uncertainty increases over time. The most difficult industries are those with very long innovation timescales and relatively high uncertainty about the future competitive environment. The example of off-shore oil and gas exploration and extraction in the previous section illustrates the uncertainty created by the political and economic environment, in an industry requiring long-term commitments to R&D. In Book 2 we had the example of British Gas in 1996, stuck in a classical contract for natural gas when deregulation had created a spot market.

The accounting conventions of discounted cashflow (or net present value) seek to enable organisations to place a value on investment based on expected future returns. In the innovation context these conventions may be inappropriate because of the lack of any certainty of project success or future markets or prices. This is one reason why investments in R&D are often described as *options*, since they do not offer direct returns and their value is in the option to invest in products or processes that may arise from the R&D. Although assumptions about the degree of risk can be factored in, these are modelling conventions rather than reliable predictions, as the experiences of many innovation projects, such as nuclear power generation and the channel tunnel, illustrate.

Discussion of risk-taking in relation to innovation inevitably raises the issue of entrepreneurship. In Section 2 we discussed Schumpeter's view that the high risks associated with investment in innovation required individuals with exceptional characteristics. Innovation was not the domain of ordinary investors or managers, but was dependent on the heroic actions of the entrepreneurs. It is a triumph 'not of intellect but of will' in taking risks in pursuit of opportunities for superior profits. These profits accrue because of *first mover advantages* – the competitive advantage resulting from being first to the market. Such profits are inevitably temporary, as imitators follow the leading risk takers and create a bandwagon effect. As markets become established, risk reduces, and with it the degree of heroism required. So too, the opportunity for superior profits declines as more entrants begin to compete. The swarm of imitators cannot hope to match the levels of profits of the first entrants, unless they can improve the innovation, or bring some other source of competitive advantage to bear.

Entrepreneurial investment in innovation is therefore characterised by high risks, a high chance of failure, and the possibility of high profits. Significantly, Schumpeter's later work (1943) downplayed the importance of the entrepreneur as his analysis began to take the increasing importance of corporate R&D into account as a source of innovation. The cost of R&D and the need for sufficient scale and resources devoted to it reduced the opportunities for participation by entrepreneurial start-up organisations. However, as we saw in relation to biotechnology in Section 3.2.1, even in industries dominated by large corporate R&D expenditure on innovation, radical changes present opportunities for smaller companies.

All investment decisions take place within the context of organisational, national and international financial systems. These condition the patterns of investment in innovation in any organisation. Financial systems may inhibit investment in innovation in four ways, according to Tylecote (1994):

1. High interest rates *may create expensive money.*

2. Setting the effective cost of investment in innovation well above the general cost of capital *may discriminate against innovation.* Large firms often suffer such discrimination for innovating, often through reductions in their share price.

3. A time rate of discount above the effective cost of capital *may induce short-termism in firms.* Shareholder or stock market influence may operate here through a fall in the share price which would make equity funds more expensive and expose the firm to the danger of a hostile takeover bid.

4. Managerial inability or unwillingness to overcome resistance to change which would be in the interest of shareholders, creates conservatism. This depends on the extent of organisational trauma which the required innovation would involve, and on existing organisational culture.

Activity 3.3

What do these negative factors imply for strategies to *promote* investment in innovation? What key strategic measures does this suggest can be taken within organisations?

Discussion

These negatives can be turned around to suggest several ways in which innovation can be encouraged by financial systems: the provision of preferential interest rates for innovation; inducements for long-termism; and support for innovative management. At the level of the organisation, the key factors seem to be information flows, relationships between the organisation and its investors, and the creation of an innovative culture.

Of course, countries vary greatly in their macro-economic investment environments, and in the institutional relationships within which business operates. Tylecote differentiates between the *bank-based* investment environments of the continental European countries, together with Japan, Korea and Taiwan; and the *stock-exchange-based* economies of the Anglo-Saxon countries. The bank-based investment systems appeared to perform better over the previous 40 years because of the closer relationship between investor (the banks) and the firm. This created immunity from short-termism. However, the USA has been more successful than the UK and the bank-based economies in the provision of venture capital for high-risk start-up companies. More recently also, the bank-based models, particularly in Germany and Japan, have been criticised both for their inflexibility and for the increased risk they represent to dependent organisations when the banks themselves become unstable, as in the 1990s in Japan and most of the "tiger" economies of South Asia.

Investment in innovation presents management with a strategic dilemma of flexibility versus stability – the need for strategy to be responsive to the market, whilst at the same time needing to insulate investment in long-term innovation strategies from short-term financial criteria and the present demands of the market. In Section 5 of this book we look at some strategies for dealing with this dilemma.

3.5 STRATEGIC OPTIONS

Freeman (1992) identifies six principal strategies in relation to technological innovation:

- offensive
- defensive
- imitative
- dependent
- traditional
- opportunist.

The first three are all clearly different strategies for seeking advantage from innovation. The other three are effectively strategies for coping with innovation taking place elsewhere, or may be a result of specific industry context and characteristics to which organisations respond.

Offensive innovation strategy – Achieving technical and market leadership by being ahead of competitors in the introduction of new products. This requires the organisation to be knowledge-intensive, with a major commitment to R&D, and employ a high proportion of staff with scientific and technological skills. It also requires the organisation to be able to respond quickly to the confluence of technological and market opportunities.

Defensive innovation strategy – A strategy adopted where the organisation does not want to be first in the field, but neither does it want to be left behind by technical progress. The defensive innovator does not usually aim to copy the innovation of the offensive innovator – rather they will seek to differentiate their product, and often improve the original, benefiting from the market-leading path broken by the offensive innovator. This often gives the defensive innovator an advantage in the longer term (such as Boeing in early jet airliners, Matsushita in consumer electronics). You will recall the example of Zantac in the mini-case in Book 1. Here Glaxo succeeded in capturing the largest slice of the anti-ulcer drug market from the established Tagamet with its differentiated product Zantac.

Imitative innovation strategy – The imitative innovator is content with following behind the leaders in any given technology and product market, often with significant time-lags. Imitators may take out licenses from the patent-holders, and will rely on the technological advances of others.

Dependent strategy – This assumes the acceptance of a subordinate role in relation to the firms at or nearer to the leading edge. Such firms may be satellites to larger organisations, or subcontractors. They rely heavily on their customers to supply specifications and upgrade their know-how and technology.

Traditional strategy – In the case of traditional strategy, the organisation sees no need to change its product because the market does not demand change, and the competition does not compel a response. Demand for their products may result directly from the lack of innovation and change – for example, Morgan cars, reproduction antiques and handicraft industries.

The Morgan sports car, an example of a successful traditional strategy.

Opportunist strategy – Where the firm or imaginative entrepreneur identifies some opportunity in a rapidly changing market. This may not require any in-house R&D, or capability for complex design, but relies on the identification of a niche for a new product or service that nobody else has thought about.

Activity 3.4

Think about your own organisation or one with which you are familiar. Are you able to categorise its innovation strategy as offensive, defensive, imitative, dependent, traditional or opportunist? If elements of more than one of these strategic types are present in the organisation, does this suggest a lack of clear strategy?

Discussion

Our own experience in large organisations suggests that more than one strategy is often pursued in different areas. Organisations may innovate defensively in existing product markets, whilst adopting an offensive strategy in some areas. In many organisations there is likely to be a changing pattern over time, with an early offensive strategy, shifting to a defensive strategy, unless the organisation can sustain its successful offensive innovation strategy on a continuous basis (which will in turn depend on industry context). We look at the issue of sustaining innovation in mature industries in Section 4 of this book.

3.6 KEY INNOVATION SUCCESS FACTORS

A landmark study of the strategic management of innovation, which has since been repeated in many countries, was completed by the Science Policy Research Unit (SPRU) in the UK in the 1970s. SAPPHO compared pairs of innovations – one commercially successful, one unsuccessful – with the intention of identifying the factors which differentiated success from failure.

The following factors were found to discriminate between innovation success and failure:

- Successful innovators were seen to have a much better understanding of users' needs than did the unsuccessful.

- Successful innovators developed processes and structures to integrate development, production and marketing activity; failures lacked such communication between these areas.

- Successful innovators performed the development work more efficiently than the failures, but not necessarily more quickly.

- Successful innovators, although often having internal R&D capability, made use of outside technology and scientific advice; failures tended to have little communication with external knowledge sources.

- Success was correlated with high-quality R&D resources and effort dedicated to the project, and to the level of commitment in terms of team size; failures had fewer resources and lower quality products resulted.

- Success was found to be linked to the status, experience and seniority of the 'business innovator' or entrepreneur responsible for the innovation. Successful innovation champions were usually more senior and had greater authority than their counterparts in unsuccessful projects.

    (Rothwell *et al., 1974; Freeman, 1992*)

It is important to stress that *understanding users' needs* must translate into action across all functional areas. As the Sony example in Book 1 illustrated, *understanding users' needs* does not simply mean better market research. It means that R&D, design and production departments are involved with users at an early stage in the innovation process.

Rothwell (1992) summarised the main factors influencing the success of innovation which are generalisable across many sectors and industries, and which have been verified by subsequent studies. These are:

1. The establishment of good internal and external communication; effective links with external sources of scientific and technological know-how; a willingness to take on external ideas.
2. Treating innovation as a corporate task: effective functional integration; involving all departments in the project from its earliest stages; ability to design for 'makeability'.
3. Implementing careful planning and project control procedures: committing resources to early and open screening of new projects; regular appraisal of projects.
4. Efficiency in development work and high quality production: implementing effective quality control procedures; taking advantage of up-to-date production equipment.
5. Strong market orientation: emphasis on satisfying user-needs; efficient customer links; where possible, involving potential users in the development process.
6. Providing good technical service to customers, including customer training where appropriate; efficient spares supply.
7. The presence of certain key individuals: effective product champions and technological gatekeepers.
8. High quality of management: dynamic, open-minded managers; ability to attract and retain talented managers and researchers; a commitment to the development of human capital.

Rothwell emphasises that successful innovation requires organisations to build and co-ordinate capabilities across *all* functions. There are no examples of successful innovators being focused on a single factor. Although the priority between factors varies between sectors and industries, the range of factors does not. Empirical evidence also supports the view that quality of management is of paramount importance since innovation is a social process.

4 Innovation in context

We began this book by looking at the macro-economic dimensions of innovation, and Section 3 explored the characteristics of innovation and the processes that condition the success or failure of innovation in organisations. The Set Book chapter you read in connection with Section 3 focused on 'technology-intensive' organisations. Here we will further explore sectoral differences, as well as looking at innovation from the perspective of mature organisations.

4.1 INNOVATION AND THE SERVICE SECTOR

Many service-sector organisations are innovative in a great variety of ways. This applies both to organisational innovations and technological innovations since many service-sector organisations possess sophisticated in-house software and ICT systems capability.

Service-sector organisations can innovate through the strategic *application* of technology. This can be a source of advantage in all types of organisations through product or process innovation, or the combination of both. Read the mini-case on the Direct Line insurance company and consider the questions in Activity 4.1 as you read.

> ### MINI-CASE: DIRECT LINE INSURANCE
>
> Direct Line is a UK insurance company. Founded in 1985, it has experienced explosive growth in the sale of motor vehicle policies. [...]
>
> In 1990 Direct Line was one of only three motor insurance companies awarded a top rating by the consumer magazine *Which?* for its speed and efficiency in claims handling. Furthermore, it was the only leading UK motor insurer that year to report net profits on its underwriting business. [...]
>
> The concept of providing motor insurance services by telephone was proposed to the Royal Bank of Scotland by Peter Wood, an entrepreneurial former insurance broker in 1984. Direct Line was trading within eight months with Wood as its chief executive. The arrangement allowed him to operate without interference from the parent company, and by 1992 Wood had become the UK's highest paid executive.
>
> Direct Line accepts customers only by telephone so it does not have to pay commissions to traditional brokerage channels, estimated to be 25–40 per cent of the value of premiums. It also differs from the majority of the industry in other respects. It accepts payments only via bank direct debit or credit card, for example. In addition to these innovations in customer contact, Direct Line employs powerful IT systems to control costs, to speed processing of quotations and claims, to facilitate market analysis, and to exploit marketing and product opportunities rapidly. IT provides management with timely information on past underwriting experience in general and also regarding specific customers. This enables it to maximise efficiency in dealing with claims, to ensure customer satisfaction and high service quality, yet contain the costs of fraudulent claims. [...]

The firm monitors the effects of its advertising on sales and corporate image. However, Direct Line focuses not only on the *generation* of new business but also on the successful retention of current customers, an endemic problem for the industry. It has achieved a customer *retention* rate of 85 per cent versus 50 per cent for the industry as a whole. It has achieved this considerable success by providing rapid and very competitive quotations, and in the quality of its after-sales service. Senior management has been very committed to excellent after-sales service, exemplified by providing 24-hour emergency telephone lines for clients in distress – such as after an accident – and optional rescue services for vehicle breakdown. The firm also emphasises the need to give prompt approval for repair work to begin. All these services are enabled by the investment in information technology.

The ... Direct Line 'formula' has, ... arguably, transformed the UK motor insurance market. Most of the large companies have either introduced a direct writing facility or are seriously considering doing so. Meanwhile, Direct Line has moved on, entering the market for home insurance and, with support from the Royal Bank of Scotland, the provision of mortgages to existing clients. [...]

Direct Line became a subsidiary of the Royal Bank Group and Peter Wood sold his 25 per cent shareholding to the bank in return for an earnings formula based on the performance of Direct Line. In return, Wood was given a free hand to develop the business without central interference. In 1992, Wood was appointed to the board of The Royal Bank of Scotland Group.

This early period was spent in frantic development of the sophisticated communication and information systems behind Wood's idea. It was intended from the beginning to develop a direct telephone and mail distribution channel bypassing the brokerage route and thus saving the commission charged.

After the sale of the first policy there followed a period of test marketing prior to a national launch in September 1985. The business grew rapidly, driven by carefully monitored tactical press advertising and marketing to the customers of the Royal Bank. By 1992 Direct Line had grown dramatically and was the market leader in direct insurance with some 670,000 motor policy holders. This represented an increase of 89.9 per cent in premium income over 1991 while at the same time the company's expense ratio had reduced from 19.6 per cent to an industry low of 14.5 per cent. In a traditional broker-based insurance company around 38 per cent of total expenses are commission and a further 17 per cent relate to claims handling. In Direct Line some 12 per cent of expenses were variable. The remainder of the expense base was more or less fixed. Substantial scale economies would thus occur if volumes were increased to the point where capacity constraints occurred. Nevertheless, since much of Direct Line's fixed costs were based on computing and communication while labour costs were limited, substantial experience effects were possible.

In addition to its expense ratio advantage Direct Line had been successful in driving down its claims ratio to below 70 per cent compared with an industry average of over 80 per cent. This reflected the superior risk profile of Direct Line's motor portfolio. [...]

The dramatic success of Direct Line had spawned imitators. The nearest competitor was Churchill Insurance. This company, started by one of the co-founders of Direct Line and operating in a very similar manner, had been acquired by Winterthur, one of the leading Swiss insurers. Other recent 'direct writers' included Topdanmate from Denmark and Gan-Minster from France.

> The main casualties of Direct Line's success, however, were the British composite insurers who historically had sold their policies through independent brokers. [...] The success of direct writing had spurred the composites to reply with a variety of strategies. Some had responded by tightening their links with those brokers who obtained the best quality business for them. Further, they had stopped accepting policies from brokers whose business produced higher than average claims. However, the lack of sophisticated management information systems in many insurance companies made it difficult for individual companies clearly to identify the source of specific segment/broker profits or losses.
>
> Other companies had attempted to secure their channels of distribution by integrating forward into broking by acquiring interests in leading broking groups such as Swinton, AA Insurance Services and Hill House Hammond. Three companies – General Accident, Royal Insurance and Eagle Star – established their own direct writing operations between 1988 and 1990. However, these companies were anxious not to disturb their traditional broker-based channels and thus did not capitalise on the parent company's image by identifying closely with their subsidiaries. During 1991, for example, General Accident was faced with a brief boycott by brokers angered by its promotion of direct sales. The continued success of Direct Line and the other direct writers was forcing a change of attitude amongst the composites and greater recognition of the new channel seemed an essential strategy for the 1990s. [...]
>
> Direct Line was an innovative user of technology to help keep down the cost of premiums. [...] A combined effect of the level of personal service and low cost delivery systems meant that Direct Line, despite product/services imitators from the traditional service industries continued to show substantial growth throughout the 1980s and early 1990s. Moreover, via its integrated Management Information Systems (MIS), the company constantly monitored its customer base to identify claim abuse, extra policy marketing opportunities and the like and adjusted premiums based on the level of overall actuarial risk.
>
> (Source: Channon, 1996)

Activity 4.1

What is innovative about Direct Line's strategy? What are the company's core capabilities? What is their source of competitive advantage? Does this case have implications for other types of service-sector organisations, for example, in the public sector?

Discussion

Direct Line innovatively uses ICTs to provide on-line insurance services, bypassing the conventional insurance broker system and reducing costs. Their computer system not only supports on-line transactions, the MIS provides managers with analyses of the business so that they can react quickly to opportunities and threats. It also requires capabilities in human resource management and the training appropriate to delivering fast, accurate and friendly telephone responses to customers. For traditional insurance companies Direct Line represents a major threat, not only because of its lower costs and efficiency, but also because it has changed the structure of the industry by bypassing the brokers and agents, which existing companies have been reluctant (or unable, due to retaliatory action by the brokers) to do. Arguably, the broker-based system dates from a previous era when personal service and form-filling depended on customers visiting a broker's office. The traditional insurance companies had become locked into an institutional structure that new technology had made largely redundant. The central advantage that Direct Line had, therefore, was in being a new entrant, which was not locked into institutional relationships, or wedded to old working practices. We should also note that Direct Line's profitability is also due to low claims rates, which it achieves by refusing to insure higher risk categories of motorists.

Elements of the Direct Line strategy may be more widely applicable in the service and public sectors, for example, by:

- *building the capability to develop innovative ICT systems that not only support existing processes, but provide MIS that enable managers to respond to events much more quickly*
- *bypassing or eliminating outmoded procedures and institutional structures, for example, by establishing direct EDI (electronic data interchange) links between hospitals and manufacturers of medical supplies*
- *providing enhanced links between customers or users and the service supplier.*

If Direct Line's claims about response times and customer satisfaction are reliable, service sector organisations of all kinds might benefit from emulating their strategies. However, existing organisations in any sector are unlikely to be able to easily free themselves from institutional relationships. The radical changes in processes and procedures inherent in a Direct Line approach represent major threats to jobs, careers and skills. Existing players in established sectors will always be at a disadvantage with respect to innovative new entrants, as long as the barriers to new entrants are relatively low. In the case of motor insurance, Direct Line were able to base their (conservative, in terms of insurance risk) strategy on existing data, in a mature business with strong financial support from its parent bank.

We noted in Section 3 that no all-embracing generic model of innovation is likely. Understanding the differences in innovation strategies between sectors enables us to appreciate the innovation strategies of our customers, suppliers, and even competitors. These strategies may be quite different from your own organisation's because they correspond to a different sector or organisational type. Another principal way of desegregating innovative organisations is according to their size.

4.2 LARGE FIRMS, SMALL FIRMS AND INNOVATION

The debate about the relative contributions of large firms and small firms to innovation is long-running. What emerges is that although small firms have received considerable attention, there is little evidence that innovative advantage is unequivocally associated with firm size. Both large and small firms have advantages and disadvantages. The strategic advantages of small firms focus on flexibility, entrepreneurship, dynamism, learning, and responsiveness to changes of all types. They tend to make innovative contributions in sectors where entry costs are low and there are niches that they can focus on. Large firms have the strategic advantage of greater financial, technological and human resources. Some large firms have adopted a strategy of attempting to create a small firm environment within the organisation in order to gain the advantage of flexibility. This strategy – known as *intrapreneurship* – is particularly associated with the American company 3M, described briefly in the mini-case below.

> ### MINI-CASE: MASTERS OF INNOVATION: HOW 3M KEEPS ITS NEW PRODUCTS COMING
>
> Through the decades, 3M has managed to keep its creative spirit alive. The result is a company that spins out new products faster and better than just about anyone. It boasts an impressive catalog of more than 60,000 products, from Post-it notes to heart–lung machines. What's more, 32% of 3M's $10.6 billion in 1988 sales came from products introduced within the past five years. Antistatic videotape, translucent dental braces, synthetic ligaments for damaged knees, and heavy-duty reflective sheeting for construction signs are just a few of the highly profitable new products that contributed to record earnings of $1.15 billion in 1988.
>
> At a time when many big US corporations are trying to untangle themselves from bureaucracy, 3M stands apart as a smooth-running innovation machine. Along with a handful of other companies that might be called the Innovation Elite – Merck, Hewlett-Packard, and Rubbermaid among them – 3M is celebrated year after year in the rankings of most-respected companies. Business Schools across the country make 3M a case study in new-product development, and management gurus trumpet 3M's methods. Peter Drucker's *Innovation and Entrepreneurship* is peppered with 3M tales. [...]
>
> So how does 3M do it? One way is to encourage inventive zealots. [...] The scarcity of corporate rules at 3M leaves room for plenty of experimentation – and failure. [...] Salaries and promotions are tied to the successful shepherding of new products from inception to commercialization. One big carrot: the fanatical 3Mer who champions a new product out the door then gets the chance to manage it as if it were his or her own business.
>
> Since the bias is toward creating new products, anything that gets in the way, whether it's turf fights, overplanning, or the 'not-invented-here' syndrome, is quickly stamped out. Divisions are kept small, on average about $200 million in sales, and they are expected to share knowledge and manpower. In fact, informal information-sharing sessions spring up willy-nilly at 3M – in the scores of laboratories and small meeting rooms or in the hallways. And it's not unusual for customers to be involved in these brainstorming klatches.
>
> That's not to say that corporate restraint is non-existent. 3Mers tend to be self-policing. Sure, there are financial measures that a new-product team must meet to proceed to different stages of development, but the real control lies in constant peer review and feedback.
>
> The cultural rules work – and go a long way toward explaining why an old-line manufacturing company, whose base products are sandpaper and tape, has become a master at innovation. And a highly profitable one at that. [...]
>
> Here's how it typically works: a 3Mer comes up with an idea for a new product. He or she forms an action team by recruiting full-time members from

technical areas, manufacturing, marketing, sales, and maybe finance. The team designs the product and figures out how to produce and market it. Then it develops new uses and line extensions. All members of the team are promoted and get raises as the project goes from hurdle to hurdle. [...]

3M Relies on a few simple rules ...

Keep divisions small. Division managers must know each staffer's first name. When a division gets too big, perhaps reaching $250 to $300 million in sales, it is split up.

Tolerate failure. By encouraging plenty of experimentation and risk-taking, there are more chances for a new-product hit. The goal: Divisions must derive 25% of sales from products introduced in the past five years. The target may be boosted to 30%.

Motivate the champions. When a 3Mer comes up with a product idea, he or she recruits an action team to develop it. Salaries and promotions are tied to the product's progress. The champion has a chance to someday run his or her own product group or division.

Stay close to the customer. Researchers, marketers, and managers visit with customers and routinely invite them to help brainstorm product ideas.

Share the wealth. Technology, wherever it's developed, belongs to everyone.

Don't kill a project. If an idea can't find a home in one of 3M's divisions, a staffer can devote 15% of his or her time to prove it is workable. For those who need seed money, as many as 90 Genesis grants of $50,000 are awarded each year.

... While other companies have their own approaches

RUBBERMAID   30% of sales must come from products developed in the past five years. Looks for fresh design ideas anywhere; now trying to apply the Ford Taurus-style soft look to garbage cans. A recent success: stackable plastic outdoor chairs.

HEWLETT-PACKARD   Researchers urged to spend 10% of time on own pet projects; 24-hour access to labs and equipment; keeps divisions small to rally the kind of spirit that produces big winners such as its LaserJet laser printer.

MERCK   Gives researchers time and resources to pursue high-risk, high-payoff products. After a major scientific journal said work on anticholesterol agents like Mevacor would likely be fruitless, Merck kept at it. The drug is a potential blockbuster.

JOHNSON & JOHNSON   The freedom to fail is a built-in cultural prerogative. Lots of autonomous operating units spur innovations such as its Acuvue disposable contact lenses.

BLACK & DECKER   Turnaround built partly on new-product push. Advisory councils get ideas from customers. Some new hot sellers: the Cordless Screwdriver and ThunderVolt, a cordless powertool that packs enough punch for heavy-duty construction work.

(Source: Mitchell, 1989)

Rothwell (1983) has argued convincingly that a complementary relationship exists between large and small firms in relation to innovation. Large firms may often be the sources of major research breakthroughs resulting from long-term commitments to R&D of the type that small firms cannot support. However, small firms are able to exploit the potential of new technologies more rapidly than traditional large firms. Often the entrepreneurial individuals who start new enterprises to exploit the potential of new technologies have themselves transferred out of the large firms that supported the long-term R&D that made these breakthroughs possible.

For large firms, the strategic challenge is to address the areas that disadvantage them in comparison with small firms. They may do this through the 3M intrapreneurial strategy, through alliances, or, as we have seen in the biotechnology example, through acquisition of the successful smaller firms. This latter strategy presents major challenges in maintaining the characteristics of the small firm that gave it strategic advantages for innovation in the first place. For small firms the challenge is to maintain control of their intellectual property to appropriate profits from it, and to maintain their innovative performance. Later books in this course address strategic alliances in greater depth.

So far in looking at innovation and strategy we have focused on new industries and entrepreneurship. However, the economies of Europe, Asia and the US are dominated by mature organisations which, if they are to continue to survive and prosper, must find ways to re-invent themselves and continue to innovate. The next section addresses the strategic challenges for these mature organisations.

4.3 INNOVATION IN MATURE INDUSTRIES

The factors that drive innovation change as industries and product-markets mature. This is partly due to intensified competition and partly due to product lifecycles. Mature organisations must find ways to sustain innovation while coping with a central dilemma: the tension between their past success and its maintenance based on cumulative capabilities, and the need to change and develop.

Activity 4.2

Now read Baden-Fuller and Stopford on mature organisations, 'Maturity is a state of mind', in the Course Reader.

As you read the article, consider what options are open to mature organisations seeking to innovate and what are the particular challenges mature organisations face.

Discussion

We discussed a case of innovation in a mature industry in the earlier mini-case on Direct Line Insurance's entry into motor insurance. The case described how Direct Line gained advantage by altering the basis of competition in the industry, and changing its structure. The discussion in the case, however, stated that, 'the central advantage that Direct Line had ... was in being a new entrant, which was not locked into institutional relationships, or wedded to old working practices.'

Baden-Fuller and Stopford's interest is not in such new entrants who can more easily break the conventions of competition. Instead, they have identified a range of existing companies operating in mature, often relatively unexciting, industries who, when faced with decline have found ways to innovate and dramatically improve their performance. They identified a number of behaviours and attitudes that were features of these 'rejuvenators'. While the innovations in question may often have involved product or process technologies, they were as likely to involve new approaches to competition, such as that described earlier in this book when Toyota introduced the just-in-time 'kanban' system in the 1950s.

Importantly, and reinforcing our conclusions in the Direct Line mini-case about the difficulties for existing competitors 'wedded to old working practices' in mature industries, their central conclusion is that 'maturity is a state of mind'. The ability to imagine a future other than one of decline was the key factor in the ability of the rejuvenators to break their institutional habits of competition.

Baden-Fuller and Stopford's analysis focuses on the business organisation and they are interested in why some organisations in an industry innovate and rejuvenate, while others do not. They very deliberately talk about mature businesses (those organisations who cannot rejuvenate), not mature industries. In this, they echo the findings of Rumelt discussed in Book 3, whose research found that only small portions of company profits could be explained by the industry effects which Porter claimed were the prime determinants of superior profitability.

After you have studied Section 4.3 you should watch the video on the offshore oil and gas exploration and production industry (Video 1 VC0864 Band 3).

As we discussed earlier in this book, this industry was driven by the collapse of the price of crude oil to develop technological processes which significantly reduce the costs of finding and developing oil reserves. The video goes further to examine how one company, BP in its Atlantic Frontier Programme, has pioneered organisational innovations which further reduce costs and encourage creative responses to technical and business problems. At the extreme, these innovations have made viable huge projects which lay dormant and underdeveloped under the old working practices of the previous twenty years.

The video and the Baden-Fuller and Stopford article describe rejuvenating businesses where managers believe that purposeful action can make a difference as to whether their organisation prospers, survives or dies. In this they also echo the introduction to the course in Book 1 where we described strategy as a purposeful activity, one where managers could make a difference through exploiting the resources and capabilities at their disposal. The capacity to pursue innovation is one of the foremost of those capabilities.

Kodama's (1995) notion of the new techno-economic paradigm, which we introduced in Section 2, has many similar features but also emphasises the creation of knowledge through greater commitments to R&D, technology fusion, inter-organisational collective learning, inter-industry competition, and the co-evolution of technology and institutions.

5 Building the capability to innovate

This book has raised a number of questions and identified a number of key challenges in thinking about strategy and innovation. In some cases these competitive challenges appear to be paradoxical:

- the need to be responsive to users' needs, but to not get too close to users, or rather, too focused on their immediate wants
- the need to pursue incremental innovation whilst remaining alert to radical innovative changes in technology, or rivals' business processes, that may undermine the position of your organisation.

In other cases the challenges are born of the complexity of systems and processes and the cross-functional (interdisciplinary) nature of the innovation process. As a result, organisations must develop the resources and capabilities to deal with a range of difficult challenges that are unlikely to go away, and indeed, are almost certain to intensify.

Activity 5.1

Give three reasons why these challenges are likely to intensify for European organisations.

Discussion

1 *increasing competition through global participation in innovation, especially at present from South East Asia, South America, India and Eastern Europe*
2 *the increasing complexity and interdisciplinary nature of technology is unlikely to diminish*
3 *The emergence/intensification of a new techno-economic paradigm which will require new organisational forms if it is to be fully exploited.*

How will organisations be able to deal with existing challenges and their intensification over the next decade? In this section we will look at the strategic management of the resources and capabilities required for innovation, and perhaps survival, in the period ahead.

5.1 INNOVATION AND ORGANISATIONAL CAPABILITY

In a recent article Baden-Fuller (1995) locates the role of innovation in strategic management. Baden-Fuller states that, although innovation plays a significant role in the established strategy literature (e.g. Chandler, 1962), it is the new dynamic resource-based or capability-based model of the firm (as discussed in Book 4) that best explains the significance of innovation in strategy. The dynamic capabilities model suggests that firms are different: they are distinguished by their ability to utilise resources in innovative ways.

In this section we examine the ways in which organisations build the capabilities necessary for innovation. In line with the major themes of this course, our approach is to emphasise the dynamic nature of capability-building as the central focus of organisational strategy. We also explore the strategies necessary for organisations to participate in the pattern of innovation that is emerging.

5.2 INNOVATION AND ORGANISATION

We have seen that Schumpeter's early entrepreneurial model of innovation, which focused on the heroic individual, gave way in the mid-twentieth century to a model based on the large corporation. Chandler (1962) documented the efficiency advantages of the divisionalised (which will be discussed more fully in Books 8, 10 and 11) in which the R&D laboratory played a major role. Corporate R&D was viewed as the locus of innovative activity, as the requirement for a significant 'critical mass' of research capability began to dominate in sectors such as electronics, pharmaceuticals, chemicals and aerospace.

As the Xerox GUI/Apple example in Book 4 showed, the divisionalised corporation with a separate R&D laboratory presented problems. Rousell *et al.* (1991) suggest that there are three generations in the history of industrial innovation in large corporations. In generation 1 there is a high wall between the R&D department and the factory. The R&D department would invent something, and throw it over the wall to the factory. In generation 2 the high wall is still there, but this time the factory write down what they want the R&D department to develop for them, and throw the message over the wall to the R&D department. In generation 3 the wall has been demolished, and the R&D and other factory departments sit down together to discuss their capabilities and common needs. The authors note, however, that generation 3 has not yet been reached by many companies.

In contrast to this picture, it is clear that innovation requires organisational structures and processes that support integration across functional areas. The provision of horizontal links between the functional areas of the firm, often involving the transfer of individuals between R&D and production, has been identified as being of key importance in the successful management of innovation.

Figure 5.1 (overleaf) shows how one electronics company plans its strategy for R&D and product innovation. The diagram shows how research is categorised according to strategic value. The left-hand scale shows how sponsorship of the research varies according to the type of R&D. The shading indicates how the company plans its R&D, and identifies those areas it avoids. The company makes a key distinction between *generic* research, which may be applicable across a range of product-markets, and product-specific research and development. Generic research is funded from central funds, which are gathered by a levy across all divisions.

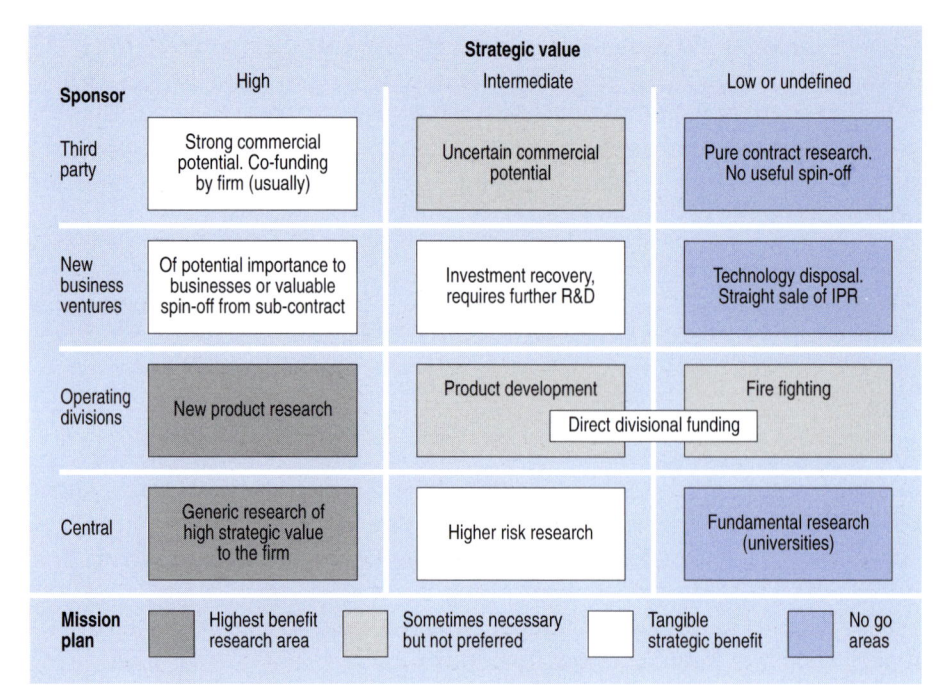

	Strategic value		
Sponsor	High	Intermediate	Low or undefined
Third party	Strong commercial potential. Co-funding by firm (usually)	Uncertain commercial potential	Pure contract research. No useful spin-off
New business ventures	Of potential importance to businesses or valuable spin-off from sub-contract	Investment recovery, requires further R&D	Technology disposal. Straight sale of IPR
Operating divisions	New product research	Product development — Direct divisional funding	Fire fighting
Central	Generic research of high strategic value to the firm	Higher risk research	Fundamental research (universities)

Mission plan: Highest benefit research area | Sometimes necessary but not preferred | Tangible strategic benefit | No go areas

Figure 5.1   R&D strategy in an electronics company

Activity 5.2

Where does the strategy in Figure 5.1 look most vulnerable?

Discussion

The strategy exemplified in Figure 5.1 shows some weakness in the area of R&D with 'uncertain commercial potential'. As we noted earlier, organisations may be vulnerable to technology that comes from outside their current expertise and R&D focus. This was illustrated by many examples, including the pharmaceuticals industry in relation to biotechnology.

One way of thinking strategically about this problem is to distinguish between *core* and *peripheral* technology. The core technology of an organisation is that which forms the basis of current activities, and therefore it is the area in which it must continually maintain a core capability. Peripheral technology is on the edge of current mainstream activity and capability. However, the problem is that technology regarded as being peripheral today may, over time, become the basis of the future core business. Organisations must find ways of tracking new technological developments whilst maintaining capabilities in their core technology areas. This presents challenges in generating the resources and developing the expertise to do this.

One way of looking at these issues, which is gaining currency, is to see the strategic management of innovation as a process of knowledge management.

5.3 INNOVATION AS KNOWLEDGE MANAGEMENT

Innovation results from inputs of all kinds of knowledge or intellectual capital, including the know-how and expertise accumulated by individuals. As we discussed in Book 4, much of this knowledge in individuals is not captured by any formal systems – it is tacit knowledge that is difficult to codify. Other forms of knowledge, such as design briefs, specifications, patents, manuals of procedures and guidelines, are written down or otherwise codified, and therefore easier to transfer between individuals, departments and organisations, or reproduced over time. Tacit knowledge is recognised as valuable, but few organisations have management tools which enable them to evaluate, grow, protect and value informal and tacit knowledge.

Organisations must find ways to orchestrate the knowledge inputs to innovation. They must decide what they need to 'own', and what they can afford to subcontract, buy in, or acquire through alliances or other means. One major requirement for innovation to occur concerns the transfer and assimilation of knowledge.

Pavitt (1989) emphasises that the cost of assimilating knowledge and technologies from outside a firm is very high. The knowledge applied by commercial enterprises tends to be firm-specific and cumulative. Corporate technological competences are built over many years through R&D and 'learning-by-doing' processes, and thus often involve tacit skills which are not easily transferable. This view has recently been confirmed in a detailed international study of the opto-electronics industry (Miyazaki, 1995).

One of the reasons why firms undertake R&D is in order to be able to track external developments and to assimilate knowledge or technology from outside the firm boundary. Cohen and Levinthal's (1989) empirical analysis confirms that R&D has a dual role: in addition to the generation of information and innovations, its function is to enable organisations to understand external developments and to learn from their environment.

This process is not only dependent on the ability of the organisation to access, assimilate and learn, but is also conditional on the types of knowledge being transferred. Much of the knowledge generated by R&D is tacit knowledge, which is difficult to transfer between organisations, as is aptly illustrated by a study of collaboration between Western and Japanese firms. Hamel *et al.* (1989) found that Western companies tended to bring easily imitated technology to a collaboration, whereas Japanese firms' strengths were often 'difficult to unravel' competences which were less transferable. As the example of the alliance between the Rover and Honda car companies has shown, it *is* possible to transfer such knowledge, but this requires very close partnerships over an extended time period.

Collaborations and alliances with other organisations in R&D consortia or joint R&D projects offer opportunities to pursue a wider spread of technologies and access a broader range of expertise than would otherwise be possible, but require experienced and cautious management. This topic of the management of alliances will be referred to in Books 10 and 11.

5.4 STRATEGIC COLLABORATION AND INNOVATION

Innovation often requires organisations to rapidly acquire new capabilities or to ensure the presence of resources that may be in scarce supply. What is lacking is the expertise to move into new areas, or to harness new technologies. The increasing complexity and interdisciplinary nature of technology has heightened the requirement for inter-organisational knowledge flows, or what Kodama calls the 'fusion' of different types of technology.

There are many examples of the need for organisations to collaborate in order to acquire new skills and expertise from outside their main areas of capability. Often, a conventional business transaction to acquire new technology from a supplier may not work, whereas a collaborative arrangement where knowledge can be shared is more appropriate. The mini-case on Kwik-Fit illustrates this.

MINI CASE: KWIK-FIT – SOUTHERN FRIED CAR SPARES

The growth of the Kwik-Fit operation in the 1970s and 1980s reflected a strategic formula which connected a new approach to servicing cars to a new definition of the market. Unlike the traditional back-street garages which offered a complete range of maintenance and repair services, Kwik-Fit focused on the so-called 'distress purchase' market of exhaust and tyre fitting. Moreover, where the back-street operators were structured around the high levels of technological uncertainty and high skill levels associated with breakdown repairs, Kwik-Fit were able to reduce the level of technological complexity through their focus on a relatively narrow range of simple services.

This segmentation of the market was based on the increasing modularity of the product technology itself, as the design of cars became increasingly oriented to the easy replacement of standardized parts. It had important implications for the design of Kwik-Fit services. First, it allowed Kwik-Fit to promote a readily identifiable, standard range of services through an extensive network of depots, thereby achieving economies of scale. The layout of each depot, with open fitting bays, service and reception areas, gave the customer a sense of control. Similarly, by specializing in simple services – just tyre and exhaust fitting originally – Kwik-Fit were able to enhance customer control by offering 'while you wait' service. Most importantly, service specialization allowed task specialization of the workforce, putting management firmly in control of the service process, and substituting cheap labour for more highly skilled mechanics.

But the advantages of customer transparency and management control also created constraints on the future growth of the business, as control complexity grew with every new depot in the network. Centralized, bureaucratic control would have created enormous central overheads and multiplied administrative inefficiencies at depot level. Recognizing that they had 'an administrative structure that was good for 50 outlets but not for 180', and which was 'beginning to creak', Kwik-Fit management looked to IT for some solutions.

After some abortive contacts with specialist computer suppliers who seemed unable to understand their needs, a chance event led Kwik-Fit management to pursue a relationship with the US fast-food chain, 'Church's Fried Chicken' – the latter having developed a computer system which seemed particularly

> suitable. Further contacts between the two companies – with one of Church's executives managing a Kwik-Fit depot for a week to understand their operations – led to the development of a similar system for Kwik-Fit. Depot managers, not programmers, helped draw up the specifications of the system.
>
> Computer terminals were installed throughout the Kwik-Fit network. These were titled MATs (management action terminals) for fear of the detrimental effect the word 'computer' might have on staff. They performed all the essential functions of a depot's administration, including quotation and invoice production, the recording of customer and banking transactions, confirmation of stock levels, and the recording of staff working hours for payroll. At the close of trading each evening, the day's transactions are polled and collated by central mainframe computers, and by 7 a.m. the next morning managers at both central and depot level have detailed management and sales information.
>
> The system effectively frees depot managers from paperwork and routine administrative tasks. When allied to a reward structure which links the pay of both fitters and managers to depot sales and costs, it turns Kwik-Fit depots into something akin to small businesses while retaining the economic and informational advantages of the large business.
>
> *Source: Gallagher and Scott (1988)*

The Kwik-Fit example illustrates one of many different forms of inter-firm collaboration that can enhance organisations' capabilities to innovate. One advantage the Kwik-Fit collaboration had is that their partners – Church's Fried Chicken – were in a completely different business sector, and so there was no competitive rivalry between the firms. What both organisations had in common was that they were *users* of information systems – this evidently enabled Church to understand Kwik-Fit's needs better than the computer specialists.

For Kwik-Fit, the transfer of Church's expertise, gained from the perspective of a user organisation rather than an IS company, appears to have been a very effective collaboration. The mini-case illustrates the difficulty of transferring knowledge. It was necessary for the Church's executive to spend a week managing a Kwik-Fit depot, in order for the executive to learn about the business. All this suggests that communicating the nature of the organisation's processes could not easily be achieved in formal ways.

However, organisations involved in innovation collaborations have to deal with a knowledge management paradox – organisational boundaries must be permeable enough to enable the internalisation of new knowledge from external sources, on both formal and informal bases, whilst, conversely, the survival of the individual firm depends on the protection of distinctive knowledge resources and unique capabilities from competitors. Managers must be aware that when they make intellectual property, knowledge and know-how available they risk losing control of its ultimate destination.

The objective of collaboration is to assimilate knowledge from external sources, pool resources, and be able to strategically apply the technology and knowledge in your own organisation (Quintas and Guy, 1995). Accessing knowledge and technology through collaborative R&D is a function of many factors, including the ability of the recipient firm to assimilate and internalise the technology and know-how, i.e. their ability to learn (Quintas and Guy, 1995).

In Book 7 we will discuss the question of learning in organisations in some detail. Here we briefly examine the implications of our discussions on innovation for individuals within organisations.

5.5 ORGANISATIONS AND INDIVIDUALS

The needs of the individual and the demands of the organisation create a tension with regard to innovation. Innovation depends on the effective management of intellectual capital – the intangible assets of skill, knowledge and information. A major part of the intellectual capital of any organisation resides within people. These are assets 'that can vanish overnight' (Stewart, 1994). Much of the innovation literature emphasises that building innovative capability is a cumulative, path-dependent process. However, paradoxically, recent years have seen an increasing number of companies outsourcing many functional areas of business and shifting from the permanent employment of staff to short-term and contract employment. There are evident contradictions between the need for organisations to strategically develop and sustain the human intellectual capital necessary for innovation, and the increasingly transient relationship between employer and employee.

A report on competitiveness (CBI-DTI, 1994) emphasised the importance of people and organisational culture for innovation: 'truly innovative companies are those which generate a culture in which people welcome change, continuous improvement and managed risk-taking'. Individuals and organisations both need to build intellectual capital. This suggests a commitment over time.

Innovation is an emergent property of organisations – the organisation needs to create an environment in which individuals can share knowledge and contribute to innovation. Research has shown that both product and process innovation is increasingly interdisciplinary, and that innovation is typically created through long-term relationships in which information and knowledge is shared (Anderson and King, 1993). However, if knowledge is a source of power, individuals may be reluctant to share it under conditions of uncertainty (Davenport, 1994). At the extreme, giving away one's knowledge and expertise may lead to personal redundancy. Accordingly, innovation may depend on the existence of a culture of trust, in which, for example, employees are confident of procedural fairness (Korine, 1995).

5.5.1 Employment strategies for innovation

Loosened contractual ties between firms and their human resources mean that the question of how a culture which is amenable to innovation can be fostered becomes particularly acute. There is a *prima facie* case that changes towards more transient employment relationships will tend to undermine organisations' capacity to innovate. Furthermore, employment strategies assume increasing relevance to innovation and advantage as competition becomes increasingly based on knowledge. While the innovation literature highlights the importance of stable, cumulative relationships for innovation, organisations, to cope with increasingly turbulent and competitive trading conditions, have introduced more contingent relationships with their employees than the relatively longer-term employment relationships of the past (Clark, G., 1992). Such moves have been seen through use of core–periphery models of employment, the outsourcing of non-core functions, and the use of part-time and temporary workers with fewer employment protection rights (Clark, T., 1993). Such contingent employment relationships contradict the conditions deemed necessary for an innovative culture to establish itself.

There is however an alternative view that organisations should move toward looser employment relationships (e.g. Miles and Snow, 1986). Stable, highly structured employment relationships have the effect of insulating employees from the market place and the imperative to change (Adams and Brock, 1986). It follows that looser employment structures may be associated with *higher* levels of innovation, because employees who are closer to customers, working in smaller business units, may become aware of their changing needs in a way in which the more insulated employees of a large corporation do not.

5.5.2 The individual's perspective

As employment patterns move away from permanent positions towards short contracts, within less stable organisational structures, individuals must think about their own re-employment prospects – for which they must build and protect their own intellectual capital. As a result, there may be tensions between the needs of individuals and the strategic needs of their current employers.

In an environment in which people do not expect to remain in a single job during a lifetime, and where people at every level of the organisation may find themselves subject to the threat of redundancy, the portfolio of skills which an individual possesses will be of prime importance in determining earning power and economic security. In general, people whose intellectual capital is in demand by employers will be more insulated from insecurity; people whose intellectual capital is not in demand will be especially vulnerable. Individuals, then, should invest in developing their intellectual capital, by developing new skills and abilities which they expect will be in greater demand in the future. But these may not be available to the company they are currently contracted to, if their relationship is based on a classical rather than a relational contract: individuals with short contracts may be reluctant to share much of their own cumulative expertise, since it is this that makes them re-employable.

Reflection

This discussion has raised a number of issues to which, at present, there are no definitive answers. How far do you consider that a strategy of encouraging looser employment ties will put at risk the organisation's ability to sustain innovation?

What suggestions do you have for strategies that may both encourage innovation in the individual and support the efficient use of resources by organisations?

6 Summary and conclusion

This book has focused on innovation as a central component of strategy and competitive advantage. We have emphasised two principal ways in which innovation is of strategic concern to all types of organisation:

1. as an external threat to organisations supplying existing products and services
2. as a source of strategic advantage for innovating organisations.

Innovation, therefore, is both a threat and an opportunity. We have emphasised the central role of innovation in transforming the organisation's environment, from product markets to industries, sectors and whole economies. We have also shown that innovation is an emergent property of organisations, and is a strategic option across sectors.

The frameworks discussed here provide a structured way of viewing innovation. Building on previous books in the course, we have emphasised the strategic importance of growing and sustaining the dynamic capabilities and resources necessary for innovation. Concepts such as technological trajectories, systems and paradigms should help to locate your own organisation's innovation strategy within a broader, structured framework. They should also help you to understand the innovation strategies of your competitors, suppliers and customers.

We have shown how organisations may derive strategic advantage from innovation in many ways: the innovation of new products, systems or services; organisational innovation; process innovation or the incorporation of technological innovations within other products and systems.

We have particularly emphasised the inter-organisational and cross-functional context of innovation, its increasingly interdisciplinary nature, and the need for structures to support cross-functional organisational processes.

Implications for strategy

- the need to be aware of innovation threats and opportunities
- the importance of learning from past practice, without being constrained by our own strategic innovation context
- managers should explicitly recognise three central dichotomies:
  - the need to maintain a current customer focus whilst being open to radical innovation
  - the need to cumulatively build core knowledge and technology whilst tracking and coping with peripheral developments
  - the need for organisational boundaries that are open to knowledge flows whilst protecting core resources and capabilities
- the advantage of seeing innovation as a strategic process of knowledge management
- the potential of information and communication technologies (ICTs) as the basis of strategic innovation in all sectors

- the need to recognise the inter-organisational context of innovation, the benefits of strategic collaboration, and the challenges in accessing and assimilating knowledge and technology from outside existing organisational boundaries
- the need to develop strategies that match the challenges of a new innovation paradigm.

7 REFERENCES

Adams, W. and Brock, J. (1986) *The Bigness Complex: industry, labour and government in the American economy,* Pantheon, New York.

Anderson, N. and King, N. (1993) 'Innovation in organisations', *International Review of Industrial and Organisational Psychology,* Vol. 8, pp. 2–34.

Baden-Fuller, C. (1995) 'Strategic innovation, corporate entrepreneurship and matching outside-in to inside-out approaches to strategy research', *British Journal of Management,* Vol. 6, Special Issue, December, pp. S3–S16.

Banbury, C.M. and Mitchell, W. (1995) 'The effect of introducing important incremental innovations on market share and business survival', *Strategic Management Journal,* Vol. 16, pp. 161–182.

Barras, R. (1986) 'Towards a theory of innovation in services', *Research Policy,* Vol. 15, No. 4, pp. 161–173.

Barras, R. (1990) 'Interactive innovation in financial and business services: the vanguard of the service revolution', *Research Policy,* Vol. 19, No. 3, pp. 215–237.

Bower, J.L. and Christensen, C.M. (1995) 'Disruptive technologies: catching the wave', *Harvard Business Review,* January–February, pp. 43–53.

CBI-DTI (1994) *Competitiveness: how the best UK companies are winning,* Department of Trade and Industry, London.

Chandler, A.D. (1962) *Strategy and Structure,* MIT Press, Cambridge MA.

Channon, D. (1996) 'Direct Line Insurance Plc: new approaches to the insurance market' in Baden-Fuller, C. and Pitt, M. (eds) *Strategic Innovation: an international casebook on strategic management,* Routledge, London.

Clark, G. (1992) 'PRP as a strategic weapon', in Bradley, K. (ed.) *Human Resource Management: people and performance,* Dartmouth Publishing, Aldershot.

Clark, T. and Clark, I. (1993) 'Personnel management and the use of executive recruitment agencies', *Human Research Management Journal,* Vol. 1, No. 1, pp. 46–62.

Cohen, W.M. and Levinthal, D.A. (1989) 'Innovation and learning: the two faces of R&D – implications for the analysis of R&D investment', *The Economic Journal,* Vol. 99 pp. 569–596.

Davenport, T.H. (1993) *Process Innovation: re-engineering work through Information Technology,* Harvard Business School Press, Boston MA.

Davenport, T.H. (1994) 'Saving IT's Soul: human centred information management', *Harvard Business Review,* March–April 1994, pp. 119–131.

David, P.A. (1975) *Technological choice, Innovations and Economic Growth,* Cambridge University Press, Cambridge.

Dosi, G. (1982) 'Technological paradigms and technological trajectories: a suggested interpretation of the determinants and directions of technical change', *Research Policy*, Vol. 11, No. 3, pp. 147–162.

Drucker, P.F. (1988) The coming of the new organisation, *Harvard Business Review* January–February, pp. 45–53.

Fahey, L. and Narayanan, V.K. (1986) *Macroenvironmental Analysis for Strategic Management*, St Paul, MN, West Publishing.

Forrest, J.E. (1991) 'Models of the process of technological innovation', *Technology Analysis and Strategic Management*, Vol. 3, No. 4, pp. 439–453.

Foster, R.N. (1986) *Innovation: the attacker's advantage*, Macmillan, London.

Freeman, C. (1982) *The Economics of Industrial Innovation* (2nd edn), Frances Pinter, London.

Freeman, C. (1992) *The Economics of Hope*, Pinter Publishers, London.

Gallagher, J.G. and Scott, R.S. (1988) *Kwik-Fit Holdings*, European Case Clearing House, Cranfield.

Graves, A. (1987) *Comparative Trends in Automotive Research and Development*, DRC Discussion Paper No. 54, Science Policy Research Unit, University of Sussex.

Hamel, G., Doz, Y.L. and Prahalad, C.K. (1989) 'Collaborate with your competitors – and win', *Harvard Business Review*, January–February pp. 133–139.

Hippel, E. von (1976) 'The dominant role of users in the scientific instrument innovation process', *Research Policy* Vol. 5 No. 3, pp. 212–239.

Imai, K., Nonaka, I. and Takeuchi, H. (1985) 'Managing the new new product development game', in Clark, K. and Hayes, R. (eds) *The Uneasy Alliance*, Harvard Business School Press, Boston, MA.

Kanter, R.M (1984) *The Change Masters: corporate entrepreneurs at work*, George Allen & Unwin, London.

Kline, S.J. (1989) *Models of Innovation and their Policy Consequences*, Report INN-4, Department of Mechanical Engineering, Stanford University, Stanford, CA.

Kodama, F. (1995) *Emerging Patterns of Innovation: sources of Japan's technological edge*, Harvard Business School Press, Boston, MA.

Korine, H. (1995) *Procedural Fairness: a key to innovation team management*, Corporate Renewal Initiative Working Paper, INSEAD, Fontainebleau.

Langrish, J., Gibbons, M., Evans, W.G. and Jevons, F.R. (1972) *Wealth from Knowledge*, Macmillan, London,

Miles, R.E. and Snow, C.C. (1986) 'Organisations: new concepts for new forms', *California Management Review*, Vol. 28, No. 3.

Mitchell, R. (1989) 'Masters of innovation: how 3M keeps its new products coming', *Business Week*, 10 April, pp. 58–63.

Miyazaki, K. (1995) *Building Competences in the Firm: lessons from Japanese and European optoelectronics*, St Martin's Press, New York.

Mumford, L. (1934) *Technics and Civilisation*, Routledge and Kegan Paul, London.

Negroponte, N. (1995) *Being Digital*, Hodder and Stoughton, London.

Nelson, R. and Winter, S. (1982) *An Evolutionary Theory of Economic Change*, Belknap Press, Cambridge, MA.

Pavitt, K. (1989) *What do we Know about the Usefulness of Science: the case for diversity*, DRC Discussion paper No. 65, Science Policy Research Unit, University of Sussex.

Pavitt, K. (1991) 'Key characteristics of the large innovating firm', *British Journal of Management* No. 2, pp. 41–50.

Pavitt, K. (1994) 'Key characteristics of large innovating firms', in Dodgson, M. and Rothwell, R., (eds) *The Handbook of Industrial Innovation*, Edward Elgar, Aldershot.

Quinn, J. B. (1986) 'Innovation and corporate strategy: managed chaos', in M. Horwich (ed.) *Technology in the Modern Corporation: a strategic perspective*, Pergamon Press, Oxford.

Quintas, P. (1994) 'Software engineering policy and practice: lessons from the Alvey Program', *Journal of Systems and Software* Vol. 24, No.1, pp. 67–89.

Quintas, P. and Guy, K. (1995) 'Collaborative, pre-competitive R&D and the firm', *Research Policy*, Vol. 24, No. 3, pp. 325–348.

Rosenberg, N, (1982) *Inside the Black Box: technology and economics*, Cambridge University Press, Cambridge.

Rothwell, R. (1983)'Innovation and firm size: a case for dynamic complementarity; or, is small really so beautiful?', *Journal of General Management*, Vol. 8, No. 3, pp. 5–25.

Rothwell, R. (1992) 'Successful industrial innovation: critical factors for the 1990s', *R&D Management*, Vol. 22, No. 3, pp. 221–239.

Rothwell, R. (1994) 'Industrial innovation: success, strategy, trends', in Dodgson, M. and Rothwell, R. (eds) (1994) *The Handbook of Industrial Innovation*, Edward Elgar, Aldershot.

Rothwell, R. *et al.* (1974) 'SAPPHO Updated – Project SAPPHO Phase 2' *Research Policy*, Vol. 3, No. 3, pp. 258–291.

Schumpeter, J. (1935) 'The analysis of economic change', *The Review of Economic Statistics*, reprinted in *Readings in Business Cycle Theory*, Blakiston, Phil, 1944.

Schumpeter, J. (1939) *Business Cycles*, 2 vols., McGraw-Hill, New York.

Schumpeter, J. (1943) *Capitalism, Socialism and Democracy*, Allen and Unwin, London.

Sharp, M. L. (1991) 'Pharmaceuticals and biotechnology: perspectives for the European industry', in Freeman, C., Sharp, M. and Walker, W. (eds) *Technology and the Future of Europe: global competition and the environment in the 1990s*, Pinter Publishers, London.

Stewart, T.A. (1994) 'Your company's most valuable asset: intellectual capital' *Fortune*, 3 October, pp. 38–33.

Tylecote, A. (1994) 'Financial systems and innovation', in Dodgson, M. and Rothwell, R, (eds) (1994) *Handbook of Industrial Innovation*, Edward Elgar, Aldershot.

Womack, J.P., Jones, D.T. and Roos, D. (1990) *The Machine that Changed the World*, Rawson Associates, New York.

Acknowledgements

Grateful acknowledgement is made to the following sources for permission to reproduce material in this book:

Text

Pages 38–40: Channon, D. 1996, 'Direct Line Insurance PLC: new approaches to the insurance market', in Baden-Fuller, C. and Pitt, M. (eds), *Strategic Innovation*, Routledge.

Figures

Figure 1.1: Foster, R. N. 1986, *Innovation: The Attacker's Advantage*, p. 141, Macmillan London Ltd; *Figure 3.1:* Sharp, M. 1991, 'Technological Trajectories and corporate strategy in the diffusion of biotechnology', in Deiaco, E., Hornell, E. and Vickeny, G. (eds), *Technology and Investment: crucial issues for the 1990s*, Pinter Publishers, London; *Figure 3.2:* Rothwell, R. 1993, 'Systems integration and networking: towards the fifth generation innovation process', *Chaire Hydro-Quebec Conference en Gestion de la Technologie*, University of Montreal, Quebec, 28 May 1993; *Figure 3.3:* Graves, A. 1987, 'Comparative trends in automotive research and development', *DRC Discussion Paper No. 54*, SPRU, University of Sussex, Brighton, UK; *Figure 5.1:* Baden-Fuller, C. 1995, 'Strategic innovations, corporate entrepreneurship and matching outside-in to inside-out approaches to strategy research', *British Journal of Management*, 6, December 1995, © 1995 by John Wiley & Sons Ltd. Reproduced by permission of John Wiley & Sons Ltd.

Tables

Table 2.1: Reprinted from *Research Policy* 15(4), August 1986, Barras, R. 1986, 'Towards a theory of innovation in services', pp. 161–173, © 1986 with kind permission from Elsevier Science – NL, Saraburgerhartstraat 25, 1055 KV Amsterdam, The Netherlands; *Table 3.1:* Kline, S. J. 1989, 'Models of innovation and their policy consequences', *Report Inn-4*, Stanford University.

Photographs

Page 11: Ford Motor Company Ltd; *page 28:* © Hagley Museum and Library; *page 35:* Morgan Motor Co. Ltd